I0605250

The Secrets of Successful Friendships

Published in 2025 by The School of Life
First published in the USA in 2025
930 High Road, London, N12 9RT

Designed and typeset by @marciamihotichstudio
Printed in Lithuania by Balto Print

A proportion of this book has appeared online at www.theschooloflife.com/articles

Every effort has been made to contact the copyright holders of the material reproduced in this book. If any have been inadvertently overlooked, the publisher will be pleased to make restitution at the earliest opportunity.

The School of Life publishes a range of books on essential topics in psychological and emotional life, including relationships, parenting, friendship, careers and fulfilment. The aim is always to help us to understand ourselves better – and thereby to grow calmer, less confused and more purposeful. Discover our full range of titles, including books for children, here:
www.theschooloflife.com/books

The School of Life also offers a comprehensive therapy service, which complements, and draws upon, our published works:
www.theschooloflife.com/therapy

www.theschooloflife.com

ISBN 978-1-916753-23-5

10 9 8 7 6 5 4 3 2 1

The Secrets of Successful Friendships

The School of Life

Contents

Introduction

1. It's meant to be easy, but it isn't

We are surrounded by reminders that friendship is central to a full and properly lived life: an advert shows us a charming group of people delighting in each other's company at a beach barbecue; a figure we admire states in an interview that the most important thing in their life is, quite simply, their group of friends; on a Monday morning, a pleasant colleague mentions the great weekend they had with a friend they have adored for two decades who is visiting from overseas; a fascinating article delves into creative friendships between artists ... It all adds up to a beguiling evocation of intimacy and warmth. In a world where conflict and selfishness so often dominate, friendship is held up as the great universally available consolation. It's a charming, moving vision of the purpose of existence. And it is also, too often, when we can bear to explore the idea, a quietly distressing and tortuous mirage.

Our own experience of friendship tends – privately and shamefully – to fall so far short of the ideal. Loneliness continues to hound us; we struggle to communicate at depth with others; we return home from parties dissatisfied and confused. We tell others that we adore them while seldom actually managing to feel more than a tepid alliance. Friendship, which clearly seems very real for others, can somehow appear not entirely available to us. We find ourselves facing questions in the privacy of our own minds that, asked by an adult, can sound painfully naive, even humiliating: how do you make a true friend? What do friends do together? Why can't I find the friends I want? And we may end up, in the middle of the night, circling a grim existential enquiry: do I actually have any real friends?

There is no need to make an already painful situation worse. We should draw consolation from a seldom-mentioned but indubitable reality: friendship is neither easy nor natural. It definitely isn't inevitable. Some of the most sensitive and intelligent people who have ever lived have lacked friends. Many of those who appear highly social in fact harbour profound feelings of communal inadequacy. A lack of friendship usually has very little to do with a deficiency of social skills. The lonely are seldom the peculiar outcasts of popular imagination. Loneliness can coexist alongside an outwardly highly cheerful and easy manner and even – paradoxically – alongside the possession of many so-called 'friends'. We can be lonely and regularly invited to parties. We can be lonely and receive a lot of messages on our birthdays. We can be lonely and feted as highly social. The lonely may hold their own brilliantly at a party; they might be married, have children and more often than not be out in the evenings. They are not the kind of people who are supposed to be lonely or indeed look bereft and forlorn. And yet they (we) are.

Fundamentally the word 'friend' is ambiguous. It points – in ordinary usage – to a pretty nice social companion, someone to share a laugh with and perhaps see once a month or so. But it also speaks to something much more tender, fundamental and emotionally sustaining: a sense that in the company of a very special person, we will at last be able to share the most vulnerable and fragile sides of ourselves and be witnessed in our true, unadorned state; we'll have the privilege of throwing off lies and deceit and be able to say what we really believe, in all its strangeness and riskiness. Another will be able to read us deeply and accurately and will be moved to compassion by our less impressive sides – and to curiosity by our quirks and passions; what is important in us will meet with what is important in them. In a grander conception of the term, friendship may be as significant and as rare as love.

This suggests that it may not be any kind of failing that is responsible for our lack of friendships, but rather an uncommon degree of ambition. We are lonely not because we can't find anyone to spend an evening with, but because we have an unusually expansive and grand idea of what friendship should be about. We are lonely because we are refusing to accept as genuine those cheap, counterfeit images of friendship promoted by a sentimental world keen to disguise the challenges of real connection. Those who feel a lack of friendship most deeply may simply be those who cleave most intensely and sincerely to its genuine promises.

When trying to imagine what true friendship might look like, it can pay to explore some of the less familiar byways of culture and history. For example, for a period in early 19th-century Europe, a particularly elevated conception of friendship came to the fore. For a time, friendship was viewed as if it might be an equal to the summits of romantic love. A person might want to die for a friend or justify their life by one.

In the 1820s, the German artist Caspar David Friedrich painted two men seen from behind, standing alone together on a wooded hill late at night; one lays his arm comfortably on the other's shoulder. It's clearly an intimate scene. What are they doing? Are they plotting a revolution or the robbery of a local manor house? Is the official title – *Two Men Contemplating the Moon* – just cultural cover for the portrayal of a clandestine erotic liaison?

Caspar David Friedrich, *Two Men Contemplating the Moon*, c. 1825–1830

In fact, Friedrich was commemorating in art an especially intense, kind, sustaining friendship he'd had with a fellow painter, August Heinrich, who had died – at the age of only 25 – from a lung disease a few years before. He and Heinrich had discussed their craft for many hours; they had sung songs, read each other poetry, shared their dissatisfactions with society and pledged to support and care for one another for life. They had also often gone out and looked at the moon together and bonded over its solemn majesty.

This starts to hint to us what a true friendship might involve. With a real friend, we might reveal our excitements at small, unheralded but deeply significant things (it could be a love of the night sky, or of a certain kind of music, craft beer or needlework). With a real friend, we might feel as uninhibited as a child around a loving parent. Our souls might thrum in harmony. We might lay a hand or arm on theirs (without anything sensual being meant thereby). We might want to see them all the time – and even decide to live with them permanently. We might want to share every movement, large or small, of our minds.

We are – here – very far from the idea of friendship as a form of casual bonhomie. Something close to romantic is at stake, and yet it is happening independently of sex. It's a love not of the body but of the mind and spirit.

Oddly, this vision of friendship can seem to be an affront to social convention. Friendship is often represented as a form of collective chumminess: a group of people horsing around, being part of a fashionable crowd. To love the company of one or two people can appear to demote the gang. Real friends can cast a slightly humiliating shadow on what typically, but inadequately, passes for friendship. A culture that wants to promote the notion of having dozens of friends can't engage with a longing to exit a wide circle and be alone to do something serious and purposeful with just a few special others.

The best friendships are typically thought of as a matter of luck: one just happens to meet and click with the perfect friend. The classic point of reference for this comes in an essay by the 16th-century French philosopher Montaigne. In his 20s Montaigne met – quite by chance at a large party – a young lawyer by the name of Étienne de La Boétie. They immediately became 'extraordinary' friends and this lasted, unchanged, until de La Boétie's miserably early death a decade later. 'Why were we such good friends?' Montaigne asked himself in a famous essay on friendship. 'Because it was him, because it was me' was his unforgettable, tender response. But it is also a very unhelpful answer, for it announces, with intellectual elegance, a passive mystic stance. Do you want a great friend? –

Montaigne seems to be asking. Then wait and hope. There's nothing to be done except, perhaps, cross one's fingers.

Our enquiry is more hopeful. We want to replace mystery with logic. True friendship is a skill, not a piece of divine inspiration. Those who find it are not simply lucky: they understand certain crucial ideas; they are guided by specific insights into themselves and other people. And these ideas and insights can be explained and described in precise ways. We don't have to be born with innate talents for being, or making, a good friend; the capacities can be acquired via the right kind of education. Around friendship we are still, collectively, at the beginning of the kind of frank and constructive conversations we require. Our culture has long evoked the joys of having friends; we now need to talk with greater determination and vulnerability about the delicate and subtle art of making them.

2. Why the lonely are especially ready for friendship

There's a disconcerting paradox at the centre of our relationships with other people. The individual who most values, and is best capable of, deep friendship is highly likely to be a veteran of isolation, and perhaps of loneliness too. Those best suited for company will probably have spent a lot of time by themselves.

It sounds bizarre. How could someone truly fitted for friendship not be an easy social mixer? How could the capacity to get on well with other individuals lead to isolation? But in fact there are important contrasts – and even a fundamental opposition – between the characteristics that lead to social success and the attitudes that facilitate true friendship.

Let's conduct a small thought experiment. Imagine it's a Friday evening and we've been invited to a great party. Attractive people are chatting and laughing in large groups and waving to each other across the room; there's music, plenty of wine and delightful canapés; some people are starting to dance. Imagine, too, that we've come here as true friendship-seekers; we are, in the background, seeking a rare communion of souls. How would we get on? When we're introduced to someone, we might want to know who they really are. We'd ideally get them to respond to dozens of questions, many of them about their childhoods, their fears, their secret proclivities and their private hesitations. We would want to enter imaginatively into their reality, in all its joys and sorrows. This might sound like an essential ambition of friendship, but in the context of a party – that fulcrum of modern sociability – it threatens to come across as something close to eccentricity. Others are here to cast off the burdens of the day, not sift through the details of their complex selves. They want a pleasant time, not an encounter with their emotional challenges and underlying pains. Were we to deliver a succession of probing questions, our companions might urgently start to scan the room in search of lighter and more 'normal' guests.

Similarly, were we to begin expounding on our own experiences, we might quickly start to seem eerie or inappropriate. We'd acquire a reputation as an odd type if we embarked on a prolonged attempt to explain just why a holiday in the Languedoc, aged 15, was so decisive for our development, or why a recent divorce had left us unmoored and questioning the basis of our being.

True friendship requires time. But the star of the social world is typically quick: they get their funny remarks in faster than anyone else. They are adept at diffusing awkward silences with witticisms; they ruthlessly scan for pauses in the chat. Yet a sincere cast of mind can mean a person will – and should – struggle and stumble over the most basic questions. 'How was your day?' someone might ask, and we might fall silent for an age from a sense of the vertiginous gap between what our companions appear able to hear, and our sense of our own convoluted subjective truth ('For hours, I looked out of the window and saw the afternoon sky. I felt anxious for reasons I didn't understand. I kept on thinking about my 8th birthday party, when my aunt, who ...'). The more authentic an answer is, the longer it is likely to take to assemble itself in the workshop of our minds. We might – as devoted explorers of our psyches – require three minutes at the very least to be able to say how we are or what we do, by which time our interlocutors will have ruthlessly abandoned us by the peanuts.

That is why those of us who long most intensely for friendship can end up opting to stay at home. What renders us so good at friendship in theory is exactly what renders us so singularly unsuited in practice for a chat about the weekend or the upcoming holidays. It's not that we're inherently antisocial; it's that social life doesn't facilitate the kind of deeper interactions that would adequately honour the promises of interpersonal communion. We stay by ourselves because we feel less alone in our own company than we would in an average group of lively and cheerful partygoers.

Long acquaintance with feeling socially lost is precisely what can help us to form our characters in directions that will – eventually – render us excellent friends. Periods alone nudge us towards the sort of sustained self-explorations that busier people lack the incentive to undertake and will give our future friends plentiful original material to engage with. Our solitude will have incubated our social lives. Our views on politics or art, psychology or society will bear the imprint of days and nights spent in our own unusual company. Our positions will carry evidence of our independence. Solitude will have lent us a character.

People who already have many friends have many advantages. They are free of the self-doubt and fear that beset the solitary, but what they may lack is the ability to properly know and be known by another. We may want many things from our future friends. The most fundamental is that they should probably at some point in their lives have felt very lonely indeed.

3. Friendship as a solution to society's three great false promises

Modern society tends to suggest to us that we need three things to sustain us and lend our lives meaning and comfort: a family, a romantic relationship and a good job. It's an admirable list – but it's also, in reality, an extremely difficult one to realise and benefit from.

Take family. This should – according to the adverts – be an intense centre of kindness and warmth. It's around our families that we should best be able to be ourselves; here are the people who truly love and understand us; here are the warm-hearted beings who will protect and nurture us. Except, of course, that it is rare for us to leave our families – at the end of a holiday or on a Monday morning – without an intense sense of relief at being able to distance ourselves from the claustrophobia, disguised aggression, jealousy and meanness they have mired us in. Measured against their effect on our minds, most families are closer to agents of disintegration and irritation than they are sources of comfort or consolation.

Something similar holds true for love. Despite the promises of the songs and the films, few people disappoint us as vividly as those we set out to love. The person we come together with will almost certainly fail to be – as we had fervently aspired – a blend of helpmate, sexual partner, kindergarten teacher, cook, chauffeur, psychologist, counsellor and bank manager. Time will reveal them to be that most disappointing of realities: a human being.

Then comes work. It is sold to us as a vehicle for growth and self-enhancement. We will, through our labour, become truly ourselves. We'll find our deepest aspirations mirrored in our status. Our job will tell the world who we really are. Except that – almost always – it won't do anything other than give others a very distorted, often brutal snapshot of our technical merits. The best parts of ourselves seldom make it on to our CV.

It is against such bleakness that friendship emerges as not merely 'nice', but essential and purposeful too. It is in friendship that we stand to discover what society mischievously suggests we might locate in families, in couples and in the workplace.

Here we can find the support that our families will not give us; here we can discover the tenderness that our lovers don't normally make available; here we will find the recognition that our professional status is unlikely to lend us across a career. Friendship is critical in defending us against the unwitting meanness of the three greatest myths of modern existence.

Friendship spares us the family's demented insistence that we must get on brilliantly with certain people simply because we share certain strands of DNA. It liberates us from a lifetime of blaming ourselves for failing to see eye to eye with characters with whom we have nothing in common – if it wasn't for the arbitrary fact that they put us on the earth. Friendship recognises our hunger for love and closeness but directs our search away from the incoherencies of biological kinship.

So too with love. Friendship better honours what love aims at than love itself. It is in friendships that people can finally taste the tolerance, the kindness, the gentleness and the warmth that they may spend decades attempting fruitlessly to locate in their sexual unions. Partly this can happen because we arrive at friendships with intelligently limited hopes. We don't try to make our friends everything for us – and therefore they succeed at being at least a few very important things. Friendship ends up delivering the intimacy and security of relationships without their tendencies to jealousy, control, aggression and foul temper.

Friendship knows, too, that our jobs cannot possibly reflect who we really are – which is why true friends spend little time on what they are up to professionally. That one person has just been appointed director or, for that matter, might have been sidelined in a pay review matters little when two friends are playing table tennis in the garage or chatting on a country walk; these are not the reasons why true friends would have been drawn together in the first place.

We need friends for many reasons; one of the most persuasive is that we need them because families, love and careers simply don't work as we are assured they will.

4. A friendship audit: am I lonely?

It's highly understandable if we don't generally want to see ourselves as lonely – and would never want to admit to such a possibility in public. In our world, to be deemed lonely is to be at risk of humiliation and suspicion. Imagine if, for instance, at a job interview, one was asked to describe oneself and replied candidly: 'I feel isolated and misunderstood a lot of the time, even when I'm around people whom I call friends.' The position might swiftly go to someone else.

But we can approach the question of our loneliness from another angle. What if being lonely was actually a legitimate marker of being an interesting, emotionally sincere and thoughtful person? What if, in a world of superficial alliances, lonely was just what a more serious person tended naturally and legitimately to be? What if being lonely hinted at an ability to avoid superficiality and to build deep and intelligent bonds with select people? An admission of loneliness could then shift from being a troubling sign of social inadequacy to evidence of a noble condition and a promising future. We might – in a curious way – end up proud of our own loneliness.

With this in mind, we might take an unusual test that seeks to probe at the more dignified and generous reasons one might have for being lonely. Loneliness (rightly investigated) should provide a sketch of our potential for friendship: the path to true friendships should pass through an honest reckoning with the deeper, more secret ways we might presently be feeling rather alone.

(i) What do most of your so-called friends not understand about you?

You might have many friends, but how well aligned are they once you take off a self-protective and sentimental lens? Are there things about you that you try – tentatively and repeatedly – to hint at, but that find no encouragement? Is the laughter sometimes hollow? Is there more enthusiasm than any real grounds for it? Are there too many things about you that you wouldn't dream of mentioning? Be as specific as possible, no matter how odd or seldom-discussed the answers might seem. The challenging element here is to hold on to the longing to be understood despite a latent sadness at not being so; we can get so used to our needs not being met in certain areas that we suppress even the idea of how nice it would be if someone could see us as we really are.

(ii) Who might you turn to if you were disgraced as a result of an error on your part?

If a large slice of the world were to turn against you, would there be anyone who would continue to see you as you, and not just as the weirdo or loser that society made you out to be? And to turn the screws further: how would this person engage with the fact that – perhaps – a degree of blame really did attach to you? Who might see you as both guilty and still worthy of their great affection and kindness? Is there anyone for whom your merits could withstand the public exposure of your defects? And is there anyone you would treat with comparable compassionate grace?

(iii) Who would you be able to tell if there was a big problem in your relationship?

Society has plenty of time for the romantic troubles of those who are single or dating casually, but strikingly little for the difficulties of those who are married or cohabiting. Is there someone who you are certain would hear your distress in a spirit of deeply sympathetic patience? What if you had an affair or you suspected your partner was straying? What if love had cooled despite there being three small children in the house? Who would stay with you through the (perhaps) hours of anger, despair or remorse? With whom might you feel free enough not merely to blame your partner but also to express your own share of guilt and dismay at the pain in your couple?

(iv) With whom (if anyone) can you discuss your true insecurities or complexities around sex?

Although society – at least in certain parts of the world – likes to present itself as immensely open, it's a radically different matter when it comes to our erotic lives. Often, one may not fit a readily available template of social sympathy: it's tricky to be an elegantly attired Dean of the Business Faculty who wants to ...; a tank commander who ...; a mother of three delightful children with a longing to ... Given how judgemental people are, we might not even trust so-called close friends with the details of our true desires. And yet, at some level, we naturally wish we could be seen with tenderness around our more convoluted sensual aspects. We may even have forgotten to call this loneliness.

(v) With whom can you explore your daydreams?

Our daydreams about what our future could be are an important part of who we are – but they are characteristically detached from practical possibility and can easily sound absurd. To go into detail about a daydream – about what business we would like to start, or where we would want to live, or how our retirement might go, or what novel we'd want to write – can require a great degree of indulgence from another person: they have to be willing to enter our imaginative space, to allow that these thoughts are important to us, however whimsical or silly they may initially appear, and that something serious might one day come from a very rough and vulnerable early draft. Is there even one person with whom – and with mutual pleasure – you might dare to attempt a disclosure?

(vi) Who likes the idiot in you?

Mostly we go to great lengths to keep our stupidities and inadequacies out of sight, on the understanding that (even though we all have them) they would dismay or irritate others. But a true friend would be moved to like us more on account of what's unimpressive and not so clever about us: the things we have forgotten to do, the daft comments we have made, the inept gestures we are guilty of. Our idiocies – for our true friends – would not be fully separable from our merits. These friends would see, and be sweet to, our bursts of exuberant fun, slightly comical preoccupations and moments of gross clumsiness. Who, if anyone, can tolerate it when we are at our least mature?

(vii) Who teases you accurately?

Is there anyone who gently makes fun of you – not to hurt you but to deliver a reproach that is useful to your own development? Teasing is the best response to the inevitable fact that another who knows us well will and should spot many failings in us and, when they love us properly, should also want to point these out to us with kindness and wit. They should – with love – sublimate their irritation into gentle jokes. Getting someone to laugh at themselves is the most useful and thoughtful form that education and feedback ever take. It's a sign of being truly cared for.

★★★

These questions deliberately set the bar for friendship higher than usual. We might – having surveyed them – realise that we have very few friends indeed; perhaps even none at all. This is no matter for panic or shame. There are probably many people whom we like and who like us who don't in fact properly count as friends once we get more ambitious about what friendship should really entail. And yet having acknowledged our present loneliness, we can end up in a better position to begin the difficult but rewarding task of going out in search of the profoundly authentic connections we have until now lacked – and yet sincerely require, crave and deserve.

I.

Varieties of Friendship

We tend to think of friendship as a unitary category, but, in reality, there are a number of different kinds of friendship, each of which is specifically adapted to addressing a particular kind of loneliness. We might say that there are as many kinds of friend as there are ways of feeling isolated. What follows is a discussion of nine varieties of true friendship that track distinct ways in which two people can assist each other psychologically. We tease out the variants in a series of case studies.

1. The confessional friendship

The tennis match, as always, was a joy. In the club room – deserted at 3 p.m. on a Tuesday – Kieran and Salim are having their customary post-match glass of beer. Kieran is bracing himself. It's a tricky moment. He's been having trouble in his marriage and only last night lost his temper, shouted horribly at his partner, slammed the kitchen door and started wondering about divorce. Not that he feels justified. He's terrified it's all his fault. But can it really just be his fault? He doesn't know what to think or feel. Is his life unravelling?

At the tennis club, people are all (it seems) either happily married or happily separated. Everyone is always 'great'. And so, when Salim asks, 'How are things?', can Kieran dare to tell the truth? They've always enjoyed chatting, but they've never ventured into this kind of territory before. Can Kieran risk letting Salim know about what he is suffering? It would be such a relief to discuss it properly, and yet what if Salim was quietly horrified?

We are required to have two selves. On the one hand there's the outer, public self that we assiduously curate – based around the old-sounding but very much current notion of 'respectability': we want, and need, to come across to others as deserving of their approval. And then there's the inner self: the confusion of thoughts, feelings, impulses, longings, regrets, fears and phobias we know ourselves to be.

This gives rise to a tension that can grow to alarming proportions. The 'respectable' self has to edit out so much that is really going on, and causing trouble, below the surface. The 'respectable' self can't be open about any of the following: what sex is really like for us; the ways in which we tend to self-sabotage; the extent of our self-loathing; what we are ashamed of in our past and what we feel guilty about in the present; what our childhood was actually like and the things or people we in fact hate, in the face of a seeming social consensus that they are to be approved of or admired. The gap between who we feel ourselves to be and who we feel we have to be looms ever wider. It can feel impossible to be liked and understood at the same time.

We are always secretly scanning others, hoping to discern some hint that they may be more receptive to the less respectable (but psychologically central) parts of who we are; we make little probing initiatives – things we can back off from if need be.

Why has Kieran thought of Salim as someone who might understand? He has been touched by a kind of gentleness in his on-court rival. They're pretty evenly matched and Salim is very competitive, but when he loses he always goes out of his way to say how much he enjoyed the game; there's a delicacy to it – a desire not to sully Kieran's victory by being a sore loser. It's a microscopic hint, but it's still a hint. Here is someone who is saying it might be OK to lose; despite trying one's hardest. Failure needn't be a humiliation.

So, when Salim asks the customary 'All well?', Kieran utters the fundamental opening words of intimacy: 'Not so good, actually.' It can sound like such a tiny move and yet one might go for years without making it. He doesn't blurt everything out in one go. He tentatively mentions a difficult argument; he suggests he needs to make a decision. There's no detail, no great confession, just the quiet implication that there's so much more to be said.

For Salim, it's not entirely easy to respond. How should he meet these words? He could close it off with a polite formula of indifference: 'It'll all blow over; it always does.' But instead he takes the answering risk: he lets out a low, empathic 'mmmm' and murmurs, 'Tell me ...' And gradually Kieran begins to unfold the trauma of last night, and what led up to it.

What we forget, as we gear ourselves up to take the first confessional step, is the longing on the other side: Salim has his hidden troubles too, but he has been paralysed by fear of what his nice acquaintances might think of him if he were to be open about them. Kieran's vulnerability is a signal he's been waiting for.

Not this afternoon, but over time, Kieran's confession offers Salim permission (which he stands so much in need of) to start to confess the very different but equally real burdens he's been secretly labouring with: his estrangement from his highly successful brother; his shame at having – as he sees it – made so little of the wonderful opportunities life has offered him.

Reciprocity is psychologically crucial. It's not merely that one sees the compassion in another's face, but that one discovers that the other is just as muddled, fractured, hurt and confused as we are. The dial of normality is reset. The lonely sense of being freakishly awful is more accurately interpreted: we are simply like others are on the inside. We are suffering from a powerful illusion of what everyone else is like; and now – thanks to friendship – reality and self-perception can be more sanely aligned.

The conversation at the club was a few months ago. Kieran and Salim still love playing tennis together but relish, even more, the chance to talk at length about certain tricky things after the game.

A confessional friendship meets our need to be understood and liked at the same time.

2. The friend who balances us

Amongst the less expected of historical friendships is one that developed during the 1960s between two cultural figures who were almost crazily different: the cerebral poet T.S. Eliot and the anarchic comedian Groucho Marx.

In 1961, Eliot, who was obsessed by tradition, decorum and obscure references to Dante and was now in his 70s, wrote a fan letter to Marx – world-famous for his irreverent, slapstick humour. It was a bid for friendship. Marx responded warmly and the two became important to one another in the few years before Eliot's death.

This isn't just a matter of dated celebrity gossip. It's a moment when we can glimpse what we ourselves might be looking for in friendship. There's a huge tendency to assume that friends are like one another; that we want and need to be around those who share our experiences and our outlook. But Eliot and Marx are charting a different approach. Philosophically, the question is: why might we want and need to be friends with those who aren't like us at all? An answer lies in a submerged problem of every life: the extent to which we become one-sided and over-invest in a part of our nature at the expense of our true potential. We may seek in friendship to correct our imbalances of character; to locate in another the missing piece of ourselves.

Right: Groucho Marx at a press conference, 1964
Below: T.S. Eliot, c. 1959

Groucho (born in Manhattan in 1890) had, in his difficult, financially strained childhood, wished to become a doctor – that is, to master the most socially respected body of knowledge he could imagine. In fact, he had to leave school at the age of 12 to help support his family.

Tom (the 'T' *in* T.S.) *was born into a distinguished and wealthy family, in which high intellectual achievement was a central path to recognition and acceptance. He was often ill as a child and – though he may have wanted to run around and be naughty – he spent most of his time sitting quietly and reading.*

The inner specialisation we feel psychologically required to undertake leaves many aspects of who we might be undeveloped. We are, in fact, stunted, though the world may be very ready to reward the limited, constrained guise we have adopted.

Marx's delirious capacity to render everything absurd was nothing like the whole of who he was, just as Eliot's refined presentation was only an aspect, brilliantly developed, of who he might have been. In friendship Tom and Groucho were looking for balance. They were seeking to reconnect with the parts of their personalities that had been neglected or sacrificed in the pursuit of success.

We can even see the problem in their art – great as it is in both cases. Eliot really would be an even greater poet, and a more powerful force in the world today, if he could have more surely inhabited the normal ground of unrefined, unerudite experience: Marx's home territory. His specialisation in obscure references perhaps weakened rather than strengthened his poetic talent. And Groucho may have less to say to us today because pure physical comedy, to which he gave so much of his life, grows stale, while his evident capacity for the witty skewering of difficult truths ('I don't want to belong to any club that will accept me as a member') was occasional and scattered.

We're not great poets or hugely successful comic actors, but in our own way we may suffer the same kind of trouble: we too lack balance in our lives. We're hard-working at the expense of enjoying life; we're hedonistic to the detriment of our careers and relationships; we're hyper-responsible (which ends up annoying lots of people) or not responsible enough (with the same result). We're not to be blamed. We don't have to punish ourselves more for our internal biases, though we might long to find an exit from them.

It's not weird, therefore, that there can be a draw in friendship to those who, ostensibly, are so different from us; we see in them, if only in the dimmest outline, the needed correction to our own one-sidedness. The slightly brutal irony is that society tends to be suspicious of such friendships: its vision is that like should comport with like. The person in their 70s may hugely value a friendship with someone in their 30s – and vice versa – because each finds in the other a counter-force to their own anxieties. The older person is returned (despite all their fears) to a sense of relevance; the younger is given a much-needed longer perspective. But the world doesn't openly welcome such connections and in no way is set up to foster them.

Someone who is quite shy could perhaps find no better friend than another who is very confident socially – someone, that is, to correct their exaggerated anxiety around others. And the devoted socialite might rather urgently need a friend to understand, appreciate and encourage their quieter, more thoughtful side. But often we can't even imagine this happening. It's one of the tragic misapprehensions of existence: we assume that others are looking for more of the same. There's a pervasive reluctance to think that poor and rich, left and right, scientist and artist, super-sporty and elegantly languid might – at the level of friendship – crave one another.

If, like T.S. Eliot, we were to take the first step and write a fan letter to a very unexpected (but psychologically needed) person, who might it be? Who would it be lovely to be friends with not because they are like us but because they supply what's missing in us?

We pretty much always know – secretly – the excessive price we've paid to survive; we know where our imbalances lie, though self-respect may make us reluctant to own up to them. But what specifically is suppressed? What's missing? Typically it is the opposite of what we're good at. This isn't an attack on our merits but a reminder of the excess cost we paid in acquiring our specialised excellence. We're finely diplomatic because we've slightly run away from being (at times when it's needed) more directly confrontational. We're so ambitious because we're hiding our longing to be cherished for our own sake. The different other comes in as the friend of the abandoned parts of who we are.

Groucho and Tom were sketching the outline of a better world, achieved through a better psychological balance in ourselves. As it happens, they didn't entirely pull it off. In the end, they slightly irritated each other. But the value of their example doesn't lie in them getting it perfectly right. They are showing us what we long for.

A balancing friendship meets our need to discover in another the missing parts of ourselves.

3. The friend who teases us

Nadia, as happens not infrequently, has just texted to suggest a different nearby place to meet – and to announce she's running 'circa twenty-seven minutes late'. It's not literally unbearable of course, but it does irk Ilya, even though he's very fond of her. So, he texts her back …

Let's home in on a peculiar – and significant – problem with being human: we're thin-skinned. We hate being criticised. We can't stand having our defects pointed out directly. Yet, so obviously, we all have defects that we're not good at detecting for ourselves but that others can instantly spot. Inevitably, there are harder truths we need to hear. Together these two facts create one of the most maddening paradoxes of the human condition: there are really important, difficult things we should understand about ourselves and that we are really bad at taking on board and doing anything about.

Ilya writes: Very dear Madame Turgenev, I'll be so honoured to greet your beautiful spirit whenever it alights in any cocktail bar on planet Earth.

Teasing at its immature worst means mocking things another can't do anything about. But there's a more artful, adult version, in which humour is recruited to sweeten the task of correction.

This is one of the great works of friendship. Teasing, between friends, responds to the huge moral conundrum: how to deliver an awkward truth in a pleasant way; how to get the target of a criticism to embrace a lesson without feeling humiliated.

Nadia will understand. She and Ilya were both fans of Turgenev's novels when they studied together in Grenoble; the celebrated 19th-century writer was notoriously hard to pin down for social occasions and had a habit of being late for everything. But at the same time it's not really very hurtful to be compared (even in a failing) to one of the finest literary stylists of, as they like to call it, the Bourgeois Epoch.

One doesn't say, 'You are awful.' That gets nowhere. And yet the objection must be launched. Ideal teasing wraps the critical barb not in flattery but in authentic appreciation. It finds the point of reference that's alluring to the other but that can still communicate dissatisfaction. The best teasers make their affection for, and appreciative understanding of, us entirely plain in the same breath as they pinpoint a failing. The best teasing is mutual.

Ilya – it can be fairly said – sometimes shies away from stating clearly what he thinks; if Nadia asks him what he thought of a film or a book, he'll hedge his reply; she'd love him to be a little more forthright. It's not horrendous, but it's annoying to Nadia, because she really wants to meet his authentic views. At such moments she's taken to calling him the Professor of Prevarication. The barb – stop beating about the bush – is enfolded in the playful intellectual flattery of a high-sounding academic title; he's enticed to greater directness rather than shamed for his diffidence.

The world is littered with the corpses of friendships that died because two people couldn't tease one another effectively. In utopia, 'how to tease well' would be one of the key areas of academic study and of education.

A teasing friendship meets our need to find someone who can alert us to small but real defects without hurting us so much that we run away.

4. The occasional friend

Scenario one

It's just gone 11 p.m. and the last customers are leaving the restaurant. Roberto and Jamal give each other a hug after a wonderful evening and jump into different taxis. It will probably be at least a couple of weeks, and maybe longer, before they meet face to face again; they've been good friends for a few years and always relish their times together, talking intensely for three or four hours before going their separate ways.

According to Romantic ideology – as it evolved from the late 18th century onwards and has come to dominate modern thinking – friendship is a kind of failed relationship: true love means wanting to be with someone all the time. The fact that Roberto and Jamal only see each other occasionally is, by this standard, second-best. Jamal's romantically inclined sister thinks it's a great pity he never got together with Roberto and that they would have made a great couple.

Scenario two

It's just gone 11 p.m. and the last customers are leaving the restaurant. Roberto and Jamal get silently into the same taxi, heading home together. They've been married for three years; they both like the idea of going out to dinner, hoping it might rekindle some of the intensity of their early days, but often they end up just talking through the routines of domestic life or co-ordinating their diaries – and not infrequently enduring long silences, perhaps because so many matters have gradually become contentious between them.

According to a more Classical tradition of thought, one of the glories of friendship is that it is a part-time occupation. It's not merely practical limitations of time and opportunity that restrict how often Jamal and Roberto get together: there's an underlying wisdom. From the Classical perspective, what we really appreciate and delight in the other gets swamped by constant exposure to the things we don't like about each other. To be loved for what's best in us, a degree of distance may be necessary.

As friends, much of what the other is like doesn't actually matter. As friends, it's irrelevant that Roberto tends to leave milk cartons in the fridge well beyond their use-by date, though if they were together full-time, this attitude would infuriate Jamal. And Roberto doesn't care that Jamal colour-matches all his books, though he's slightly stunned to see the reality – a guide to restaurants in France next to a copy of Kant's *Critique of Pure Reason* because both happen to have red covers. And this is only to begin the list of matters over which they would contend were they to try to share the whole of their lives. Meeting only in restaurants, they can concentrate on the specific, and very real, things that delight them about one another.

In artistic terms, a friendship can be likened to a beautiful sketch. A great portraitist might capture a key aspect of someone in a few lines; it's not that they were too uncaring or too lazy to record every detail – they weren't trying to do that. They wanted to immortalise a glance, a posture, a tilt of the head, a way of gesturing. To be a friend is to be a sketching artist: it is to select out of all the things one could concentrate on what it is best to concentrate on.

It has to be admitted, though, that even in the limited arena of a restaurant encounter, with the comforts of a langoustine salad and a glass of Chablis, there are still irritants. Roberto winces slightly at the sight of Jamal's floral shirt and Jamal has to hold his tongue when Roberto mentions, in all seriousness, someone's star sign.

There's a rather specific character to minor irritants: their power to drive us crazy depends on their frequency. A small frustration stays just that – small and bearable – if it is met only at well-spaced intervals. The problem is constant repetition. An occasional gust makes a tree bend, but then it comes back into shape and continues to grow upright; a constant wind distorts the entire structure.

In the two or three weeks they have apart, Jamal and Roberto easily regain their mental suppleness and can meet afresh. Neither is overburdened, or hurt, by the shortcomings of the other. They can afford to overlook a small failing (as each sees it) to which they are rarely exposed.

Their friendship is deeply important to both of them – one of the loveliest things in their lives. And yet they have maintained their love for each other so well and for so long because their encounters are brief, occasional and intensely apprehended.

An occasional friendship meets our need to be loved for our own merits, without our failings getting in the way.

5. The thinking friend

There's a routine that Niamh and Ian have. Every Wednesday, Niamh travels across the city to knock on Ian's door around 7 p.m. Niamh does the supper; always simple, always more or less the same. The menu, however, isn't the point. They meet like this because over the next few hours they will do something that – in both their experience – is painfully rare: think together.

What makes it even more strange is *what* they think about. They don't wrestle with prestigious intellectual problems: how does the material brain generate the first-person experience of consciousness? Or, how can the theories of quantum mechanics and general relativity be reconciled? Rather they think together about seemingly minor issues.

A whole evening might be devoted to thinking through what's nice about driving at night or why Joan Armatrading's 'Heaven' is so moving. They might think about what makes for a genuinely good holiday or why Noga, a mutual acquaintance, is so hard to get on with. These might not be academically prestigious lines of enquiry (no university departments are devoted to studying them); they just happen to be highly relevant to the lives of Niamh and Ian.

Such matters sound pretty simple. But they are strangely hard to get to grips with. The answers seem easy – until one tries to spell them out to another person. Our brains, in fact, are far from perfect thinking machines; they are beset by various flaws, and the role of the thinking friend is to help us overcome these obstacles. For one thing, there's a huge tendency to rely on words that express enthusiasm (or rejection). We say, 'That was great', 'lovely', 'so nice', 'quite boring', 'so annoying', etc., but we give no detail: what actually about that thing (or person) is lovely or awful? And why does it, or do they, have this particular effect on us, given that they don't strike everyone as they strike us? The thinking friend pushes for clarification. Their desire to know more about our experience – to understand its granular character and the personal reasons behind it – is the stimulus we need to go into detail. And when we do, we discover ourselves. The thinking friend doesn't combat our opinions and responses; they want to understand them deeply.

Then, the mind has an ingrained habit of wandering off topic: talking about one thing makes us think of something else, which jogs our memory about yet another thing. We may have started off talking about why a passage in a novel is so moving, and two minutes later we're onto an anecdote about self-service checkouts at the supermarket. Without embarrassment, the thinking friend pulls us back into focus.

We're not offended, we're happy to return, but we needed their pleasant but precise reminder.

The thinking friend helps us overcome the natural, and debilitating, tendency of the mind to stay within certain self-imposed limits: we have a hypersensitivity around what we are or are not supposed to think, which blocks the path to what could be our more productive insights. Timidity disguises itself. An individual who seems intellectually very confident and bold may be constantly shying away from simpler, more straightforward ideas – even when these are really quite sensible and wise.

The joy of the thinking friend is that their (inevitable) mental timidity isn't the same as ours. They can spot when our thinking is being driven by a determination to arrive at a predetermined and, to us, safe conclusion. It's their company that makes us feel we could risk thinking differently.

And they keep us going when, left on our own, we'd simply give up. A basic principle is that the mind panics when a task seems to be taking longer than it should. A car trip that was supposed to take half an hour becomes a nightmare if we're still on the road after four hours. But with a lot of things, we have no realistic sense of how long they 'should' take. Should it take five seconds – or five hours – to work out why you find a painting charming? The thinking friend encourages us to keep going (and we them). They project the sense that it is worth continuing to wrestle, expand, clarify, revise, summarise, revise again. In their company the task is allowed to be as demanding as it really is.

It's crucial that it's a *friend* we are thinking with: we need their curiosity about us, their desire to understand us, their enthusiasm for what we might discover and their esteem even while we are struggling to articulate our ideas. The cumulative result – after months and years of thinking together – is a deeper engagement with our own thoughts and feelings; a sharper, more evolved sense of what we really think and feel, want and need, care about and like.

A thinking friendship meets our need for another to care enough about our emerging ideas to help us know our own minds.

6. Microfriendships

In the large block of apartments, Ester occasionally bumps into Shanaya in the lift. In a formal sense they're not properly friends: they haven't been in each other's homes; they don't know each other's history. But they always smile warmly, say hello and ask how the other is getting on – even if they know that the answer will have to be squeezed into the few moments it takes for the elevator to reach the ground floor.

Taking time to have small chats about nothing in particular with people we don't know and may not ever get to know fully can – from some perspectives – seem like the height of absurdity. Maybe we're in a coffee shop and someone is preparing us a drink. Or we're on a train, waiting for the doors to open. Why would we bother to hold up our day for a few moments, given how many things we already need to do and how many good friends we have who we haven't seen in far too long? We may also have a more high-minded defence for our silence: we aspire to be profound people and there is no way that we can get anywhere meaningful with a near or complete stranger in a compressed amount of time. We shun the smaller chats because – in the back of our minds – we tell ourselves that we are already deeply committed to the long and consequential ones.

But this is to miss the point – and the opportunities – presented by minor social exchanges. They stand, in relation to lengthy friendships, rather as haikus do next to 1,000-page novels; there are things a tiny poem can do that a comprehensive narrative will miss. There are single sentences that can mark us as much as entire volumes. There are pictures that can stick with us in a way that a three-hour film won't. We can be disproportionately and yet powerfully touched by so-called minor things.

When Shanaya says she's fine, there's a look on her face and a tone in her voice that communicates a great deal more; the way she says 'all is well' really means: 'I'm OK, but I know how complex life really is. OK will do as a summary, but I'm so aware of the hidden complexities in my life and, I guess, in yours too.' And Ester can hear – and appreciate – the wider resonance. They may never elaborate beyond this, but some important acknowledgement has passed between them.

Small, sympathetic chats matter above all because few of us are ever very far from sadness and despondency. There are so many reasons to dislike ourselves, to be paranoid about what other people think and to regret mistakes we've made. When we are in a febrile or fragile mood, a short, kindly exchange can be all that is needed to start turning around a deeply dark day. An enormous amount of sympathy and fellow-feeling can be compressed in the most minuscule dialogue. 'They make them like that to torture us, don't they?' we might say to a parent struggling to close the zip on a child's jacket in a sudden downpour, thereby sending a modest sign that we know how difficult things can be – and that we have in some ways been there, or somewhere like there – ourselves.

Or we might, on our way to a station, exchange one or two sympathetic words with a taxi driver about their elderly mother who, we learn, has just gone into a care home after having a fall. The chat won't change anything in an already tricky situation, but the humanity on display might notch up another argument for hope. The philosopher Arthur Schopenhauer observed that we can never know for sure who around us may, at any particular moment, be thinking of ending their own life. The thought usefully puts into relief what might be at stake in any exchange; we may – at points and without any obvious warning – be the last barrier between someone and a decision to despair.

A charge often made against small chats is that we can surely only ever be pretending to be friendly. Yet this is to miss out how much, and how deeply, our hearts may go out to people whose lives we merely brush against. We can imagine our way into pains whose details we will never know. We can – paradoxical though it sounds – love a stranger. And, even more oddly, for only a minute or two.

We are so often held back by unhelpfully grand ideas of what it means to change the world. We imagine the requirements for improvement on such a large scale that, along the way, we end up grievously neglecting what it is actually in our powers to achieve right now, today, the next time we are out. We suffer from an upside-down view of where significance can lie. We are assembled out of small things – and may live or die by their presence or absence. We have in our hands a very potent weapon already: the power to say a warm, gentle, sympathetic hello.

A microfriendship meets our need to sense that our complex humanity can be recognised by complete strangers.

7. A friend to be silly with

Jasmine and Sigrid have a particular game that's been evolving for a while between them; it started when Jasmine had been binge-watching Pingu, the TV programme about a little penguin who speaks a fabulous made-up language, with her daughter. Now the two 40-year-olds have immensely serious-seeming discussions in their own version of nonsense. The topic will be something like the first moon landing. Full of nail-biting intensity, Sigrid will do the countdown – botti, sin, solo, weewoo – then theatrical awe – strodo tintoe, leepa leepa proudy fleebydom.

A problematic point that needs to be admitted from the start is that we are all in our hearts irremediably silly. We are lots of other things too: serious, noble-minded, generous, hard-working, loyal, intelligent ... and yet all the time we are on the verge of damaging everything (in our own eyes) thanks to the occasional but massive eruption of our essential idiocy. One said that to someone at a party; one walked straight into a glass door; one says 'one' idiotically often. We are so aware of our own foolishness. We are so grievously cut off from that of others.

Today Jasmine (divorce lawyer) and Sigrid (hydraulics engineer) are mock-analysing Wittgenstein's later philosophy. It calls for frowning stares as they wrestle with huge assertions: weary job fog, chatty nainai [agonised pause to confront the imaginary insight] chimp dump sinner ordo poop shack. It's all terribly silly – and a delightful bond.

The silly and the serious are not, as we tend to suppose, enemies. The more beautifully refined, cultured and well-presented we are, the more we need open silliness in our lives. Because, ironically, the more anxiously we guard our dignity, the more fragile it becomes. The glorious sign of security is that we know perfectly well that we can be both wise and fools at the same time. There are few sweeter things than witnessing an elegantly accommodating response to human ineptitude: the perfectly attired individual who laughs (and invites others to join in) when they spill a cocktail down their gown; the premier or president who is tender and humorous and kindly helpful when the mortified waiter drops a tray.

Behind the scenes we hold ourselves together; we keep our private madness and incapacity secret as best we can. But what we fear is that others will realise that – despite our talents and successes – we are very, very silly individuals. The ideal silly friend is someone who normally presents as serious and in control but who is willing to be idiotic with us.

Jasmine and Sigrid have taken aim at an existential target. When in a plenary address to the National Efficiency Forum Sigrid lightly mispronounces the word 'focus' (it comes out as 'fuck-us'), she's not abashed. When Jasmine, with an over-enthusiastic gesture, flicks her bundle of notes onto the floor of the district court, she reacts with good-humoured aplomb. No one now can possibly see them as more ridiculous or more nonsensical than they have – blissfully – acknowledged themselves to be.

We need the notion of inoculation. We take a manageable dose of a malady and it reinforces our capacity to cope with the worst, full version when it comes. We acknowledge, in the safety of friendship, how far we are from being the rational, perfectly capable creatures of our fantasies, and the public revelation of the inglorious truth arrives not so much as a humiliation as an extension of a familiar joke. And so, we respond to our stumbles and follies with the modest grace and good humour that is amongst the sweetest and most loveable answers to the conundrum of being human.

A silly friendship meets our need to happily acknowledge, and thus disarm, our secret understanding of our own existential idiocy.

8. The old friendship

A quarter of a century ago, Xavier and Khendra were assigned to the same halls of residence in Edinburgh; they were close friends for four years, then life took them quite separate ways. Xavier lived in London for some years; Khendra worked in many countries before making Los Angeles her home. More recently they are both back living in Scotland, though on different sides of the country; their lives are very different. Khendra, who is single, is a political advisor in the Scottish Parliament; Xavier runs a chain of wholefood shops and has recently started a family with his husband, James.

They still very much like to get together occasionally to reminisce.

Psychologically speaking, ageing is a deeply ambiguous process. We almost certainly become more competent, and we like to think we become wiser. But there is also what might be called the wisdom of youth that we stand to forget, which is why reminiscing – which can sometimes sound mawkish and delusional – deserves a philosophical rethink.

Consider the fate of probably the most prosperous artist of the 19th century, Sir John Everett Millais. In his later life he made a huge fortune; his single most commercially successful work was a painting called *Bubbles*. It shows a curly-haired little boy (in

John Everett Millais, *Bubbles*, 1886

fact, his grandson) blowing soap bubbles; it's technically very skilful, but no one can claim it's addressing anything much. It was, however, massively taken up by the large and ambitious Pears soap company as the centre of an advertising campaign. It became perhaps the best-known contemporary image in the Western world.

The problem came when, in a gesture of homage, Millais' fellow artists put up an exhibition of his early work, the best of which he hadn't seen for many years. The elderly Millais – rich, celebrated and knighted – was confronted by who he had been as an artist: less polished, more urgent, caring nothing for popularity yet eager to ennoble the public. Over the years, his early insights and aspirations had been submerged in the alluring worldliness of celebrity. His style had become smoother, but his aim was less true. He wept, it is said, in shame. Millais, we may say, had not reminisced enough. And he had, we know historically, largely broken with his old friends. He'd lost touch with what was wonderful about who he used to be.

Xavier and Khendra aren't artists, but together they are keeping the wisdom of their youth alive as they age. For this it's not sufficient merely to retell externals: the way it used to be possible to rent a student flat in the Royal Circus – now a plutocratic abode; the curious fact that there used to be more direct flights between Edinburgh and Venice, not that that particularly mattered to them then. What they do instead is push each other for psychological detail.

... Remember how you got really interested in writing poetry, and used to put quotes from who-was-it up in the kitchen? Why was that so nice? What might it have become? What would be the version of that today?

... How did you feel about your parents then? I sort of forget, but I don't recall you talking much about them. How has your perspective on them changed?

... You were so unsure about what to do. Didn't you apply to work in a bank and have ideas about living in a croft? What was going on? Can you still feel in touch with the confused parts of yourself?

... Why was it that we were thrilled to be sleeping in a flea-pit hotel in Paris? (Remember the bathroom with the door that wouldn't close?) Why can't we be excited that way now, instead of so concerned about upgrades and toiletries?

... When we cleaned up after that party (the one where Imran wore that jacket) with ABBA belting out – why was tidying up such fun?

It's not that our younger selves were perfect. But in the experiences we had then, we can find so much that is nice, complicated and interesting about our own nature – some of which may not be nearly so much in evidence today. These aspects of who we are have been pushed aside by the demands of later life, but they stand – always – to be rediscovered and reanimated. We need the old friend who was with us then and knew and shared the truths that once were more visible.

An old friendship meets our need to keep alive the best of who we used to be.

9. The ideal gang

Gustavo, who has come straight from a board meeting, is lolling on the sofa saying something to Genevieve, whose gentle face is opening into a delighted smile, while Jo – who plays acoustic guitar in a band that hasn't quite made it – is leaning over the back to share the joke. Noticing them, Frederika, engaged in telling Atticus something crucial about the philosophy of Spinoza, glances up and winks at Cynthia, knowing how she'll be touched by the sofa moment. They are all friends. Jo, who dropped out of university after three months, goes swimming with Frederika (MPhil, DPhil); years ago, Genevieve was Cynthia's favourite babysitter; Atticus is Gustavo's dance instructor. But it's best – and wonderful – when they are all together.

In films we often meet the gang in its least elegant guise: a bunch of criminals intent on a heist. But even there the allure is tangible. To find oneself part of a group of friends, so different amongst themselves but all united by deep ties of affection (and with no plan of robbery), would be utterly lovely. But it's sadly so rare; it can feel like something merely for a utopian novel, impossible in our own lives.

The ideal gang invites two questions: first, why is it so especially appealing? And, second, is there anything we can do to make it less rare? How, in other words, might we form a gang of our own?

The starting point, as so often, is to understand a fear – namely the anxiety that often grips us when two very different friends, who we know quite independently, finally meet. The worry isn't simply that they won't particularly hit it off: it's quite reasonable that not everyone is going to like everyone else. It's rather the anxiety that they will see something horrible and disturbing in each other. In the vignette with which we started – which is a disguised description of a real group of friends – Cynthia was very fond of both Gustavo and Genevieve for years but long dreaded the idea of their meeting each other. Gustavo is wealthy, sophisticated and, in a business setting, can come across not merely as decisive but as impatient and demanding. Genevieve, the former nanny, is extremely sweet-natured but rather innocent and naive. Cynthia worried Gustavo would dismiss Genevieve as a dull, timid provincial – with nothing whatever to offer anyone over about the age of 6; he'd be (Cynthia imagined) disturbed to think of her wasting her time with this unprepossessing non-entity. And Cynthia was horrified at what her beloved Genevieve might make of Gustavo: she'd be too nice to say anything nasty, but in her heart she'd be saddened and alarmed that Cynthia was keeping company with such a harsh, soulless character.

The meeting did happen, eventually, at Cynthia and Frederika's wedding. Gingerly, they sat Gustavo and Genevieve as far apart as possible. But it was incredibly touching, late in the afternoon, to see them dancing together. Gustavo was being his nicest possible self – funny, gentle, kind – and he'd clearly brought out a long-buried touch of naughtiness and daring (by her standards) in Genevieve. And this was the start of the gang.

A child's life involves many divorces, in a wider sense of the term. There was a 'divorce' between Cynthia's parents and her grandfather of whom she was very fond when she was little. He had run a double-glazing company; he was jolly, direct and, in her parent's eyes, an embarrassment. They didn't even need to say anything; Cynthia could sense her father's shame when his father praised a dinner as 'a slap-up meal', whistled to indicate surprise or took to wearing a cowboy hat. Cynthia felt she was being asked to choose: would she join her parents in their distaste of his 'vulgarity', or would she keep faith with her warm grandfather (who did occasionally call her parents snooty)?

It was this fear that resurfaced around Frederika's friend Jo. Jo wasn't at all superficially like Cynthia's grandfather – he shared a satirical attitude towards 'the posh', which in his eyes would certainly include Gustavo and, in fact, Genevieve as well. For, despite her lack of money, Genevieve has a delicacy and refinement that, Cynthia was sure, Jo would dislike. And Jo could definitely come across as rough. She saw his deep vein of tenderness – the ease with which he could be moved to tears – but many would be more struck, and turned off, by his bluntness and studded leather jacket.

But again, a miracle. Both Gustavo and Genevieve took to Jo. And then they all embraced Jo's friend Atticus and four had become six. The power of the group lies in its ability to close our emotional wounds. The kinds of people we'd learnt, very painfully, couldn't be close, turn out now – in the personae of our group of friends – to embrace one another warmly. The splits in our own soul are being cured.

Cynthia's story, however, contains a troubling element: it is highly dependent on chance. It could so very easily not have happened. She speaks, in purely secular terms, of miracles because it is essentially so improbable that Gustavo would delight in Genevieve and that both of them would take to Jo and then to Atticus. This is what explains the rarity of such groups.

To fight against randomness and chance we require art. The arts, broadly understood, are humanity's attempt to deliberately create good things rather than wait upon accident. The art of irrigation overcame dependence on random floods or down-pours; the art of construction liberated us from the sheer chance of finding a suitable cave in a convenient place; the art of poetry seeks to provide a more stable supply of eloquence and insight.

Around groups, the art in question is that of making an introduction. Usually this is an abrupt affair, hardly more than a name or a single, hopefully interesting, fact: '... from Uruguay' or '... who I met when I was an intern at Reuters'.

But properly understood, an introduction is a huge thing. At its best, and most expansive, it is the attempt to teach one person how to love another. Some of the greatest novels are attempts, on the part of the writer, to introduce us properly to, and show us how to appreciate, a character who we otherwise perhaps might not much like. The entirety of *War and Peace* can be read as an extended introduction to the central character, Pierre; as if Tolstoy were with us at a party and said, ushering forward a very stout, rather complacent-looking individual, 'I'd like you to meet my friend Pierre, who ...' and then recited the entire 1,000-plus pages of the book. And, at the end, we would be utterly delighted to embrace Pierre and take him into our hearts.

If Cynthia had thought about it, she might have tried the grand strategy of proper introduction. Right at the start, long before Gustavo and Genevieve met, she could have begun introducing them to each other. Little by little she'd have described to

Gustavo how kind Genevieve had been as she was growing up; she'd have portrayed her dignity and explained her shyness. She would have searched in Gustavo for points of emotional contact. Did he have a sweet teacher at primary school? Could he imagine how nice it was for her, when she was little Cynthia, to snuggle up to such a quietly comfortable person? She'd transmit her love for Genevieve to Gustavo. It might take months or years. And she'd do the same for him to her, gradually quieting her understandable fears of such a formidable figure. The good introduction doesn't shy away from a person's more forbidding or disturbing aspects. Rather, it makes sense of them. And so, when they were finally to meet, it wouldn't be an intensely anxious moment: it would be the joyful recognition of two people who had already learnt – from a distance – to understand the charm Cynthia saw in each and, now, to see it in the flesh for themselves.

The truth is that beautiful gangs needn't actually be as rare as they are – the right art, if we can learn it, can set us free to be happy together.

Friendships within an ideal gang meet our need to close the unnecessary distances between those we love.

II.

Enemies of Friendship

However much we long for friendship, our attempts to find it can be poignantly undermined by a series of obstacles that we still know too little about and that we do not, at a societal level, discuss as often as we should.

We consider eight different kinds of enemies of friendship.

1. An absence of shared challenges

We tend not to pay much attention to the striking fact that most of our friends are acquired at very particular stages of our lives – for example, at secondary school and university, or on long, physically demanding trips, or during our early years in a new company, or after having just had children.

What these diverse situations have in common is eventfulness. Friendships develop when things are intense, involving peril, beauty, jeopardy, drama and self-development. We cement friendships when we have to confront the same sadistic teacher who sets us too much homework; when we have to spend all night in the library cramming for an exam that threatens to determine our whole futures; when we need to negotiate a hot and chaotic bus station at the foot of the Andes; when we have to struggle together to make sense of a mysterious office hierarchy or need to figure out how to feed a newborn.

It's not inherently strange that friendships should spring up under such conditions: these are today's equivalent of primordial tasks like building shelters, hunting animals and grinding corn together. What's remarkable in the modern world is how we have forgotten the importance of activity in trying to generate friendships.

For example, the favoured locale for the nurturing of new friendships tends to be a bar or a restaurant, where we can be guaranteed to face no greater shared tasks than sipping a beer or asking for a bill. What has, in all likelihood, preceded a challenge-free Saturday evening encounter is a rush to get as much done as possible so as to clear time, as we see it, for the higher business of a quiet chat.

We've probably strenuously got all the real work out of the way in the preceding hours from a sense that we would otherwise have irreparably damaged our chances of fostering mutual sympathy. We might have spent a whole afternoon doing the laundry, being perplexed by the instructions for a flat-pack bookcase, rushing around the supermarket or dropping in on our much-loved but rather difficult mother. We might then talk about our hurdles later in the restaurant, but it rarely occurs to us to actually share these hurdles with our companions in real time.

And yet, if we were properly attuned to the preconditions of friendship, we might decide to invite our friends to meet us in the supermarket and take them on a pressured gallop down our shopping list. We would task them with helping us to find the dishwasher tablets and the paper towels; and they'd reveal to us how they balanced their weekly budget and what kind of chocolate biscuits or pretzels they were drawn to. If things were going really well, we might take them home and bond over the laundry. It can be hard to claim to know anyone before we've gone through a wash together. However interesting it can be to discuss an acclaimed new film, it may be a lot more meaningful to go through a pile of freshly tumble-dried smalls. And though it can be revealing to discuss how impossible our parents are with a friend over dinner, it is a great deal more effective to take our friend to meet this mother so that they can witness her fascinating blend of tenderness and hostility in action.

We've got things backwards. We struggle alone with the real but important business of our lives and then carve out a few deeply unrepresentative placid moments in which to survey recent events. In a wiser society, we'd set out deliberately to involve our friends in our challenges and labours. We'd create opportunities to see each other flustered, laughably frustrated or surprisingly resourceful in adversity. We would bond over small, shared wars against shopping trollies, Allen keys, wrinkled shirts and awkward family meetings. We don't need to stop talking to friends, but – if we really want to grow close – we might need, far more than we realise, also to begin urgently *doing* something with them, perhaps starting with the laundry.

2. Presumptions of normality

One of the great hurdles to developing deeper friendships is the assumption that, in order to prove acceptable to other people, we need – first and foremost – to come across as extremely normal.

It's on this basis that we devote an uncommon amount of energy to hiding away all the sides of ourselves that we feel sure would horrify and revolt other people: our hesitations, our sexual quirks, our self-doubts, our neuroses and our moments of panic and despair.

We live in a world that continues to imply that reasonable people might exist. Even as, at an intimate level, no one has ever yet met such creatures.

To acquire friends, we have to make our peace with a perhaps remarkable-sounding idea: that it is normal – and even very sensible – to find life unbearable. We have crises not because we are strangely incapable of living, but because we are – all of us – inevitably at points overwhelmed by the plain unreasonableness, cruelty, senselessness and arduousness of existence.

Real friendship is not so much threatened by disclosures of vulnerabilities and compulsions as built out of them. It is impossible to become a close friend to anyone until we have dared to induct them into our less-than-impressive aspects; until we have been brave enough to display the full scale of our waywardness and our idiocies. We may awe strangers with our strength, but it is only once we dare to present them with our frailties that we are in any position to turn them into sincere allies.

Nineteenth-century Romantic culture had a lot of time for emotional eccentricity. There was a recognition that 'genius' could at times be aligned with outbreaks of what was plainly referred to as 'madness'. Talented scientists, poets, artists or philosophers were more or less expected to lapse into the odd demented moment: they might run weeping out of meetings, try to maim themselves, mess up their finances, rant or refuse to get out of bed for a month. But no one panicked because it was understood that certain very good things about these people – their extraordinary sensitivity, authenticity, creativity and insight – would also naturally throw up some more socially uncommon periods.

The error of the analysis was only that it was too narrow. It's not in truth only scientific or artistic paragons who should be given leeway to go off the rails. We are all of us entitled to sympathetic interpretations of those less conventional instances when we

Vincent van Gogh, *Self-Portrait with Bandaged Ear*, 1889

are driven to distraction by a frenzied world and the momentous contradictions in our own natures.

Everyone is inwardly distressed. Most of us keep our potential madness at bay, but we are perfectly well aware that it is there. We should not be scared off by our own turbulence or mistakenly assume that no one could like us if – with a few precautions – one day we revealed our multifaceted reality. We should not continue to lock ourselves into our loneliness from a ruinous belief that no one could witness us and keep faith with us.

By making peace with our true selves, we will also be doing others a great favour; we will simultaneously be encouraging them to befriend their own exiled parts. A friend – in the highest sense – is a select person who is alive to, and has been allowed to see, the collapse of another's respectable facade. If we never allow this to happen, if we are immensely careful never to be exposed at our worst, we can acquire a reputation as a solid-seeming person and even be celebrated as a grand and impressive one. But we will also – paradoxically and painfully – be closing the door on one of life's most nourishing and sustaining gifts: a sense that we have been fully seen by someone and, blessedly, remain liked.

3. Shyness

One of the great errors we can fall into when we set out to make friends is to trust that the way people first present themselves to us – in those tense early moments at a party or in the workplace, in a holiday resort or a lecture hall – is the sum total of who they are.

We start to get shy and unnecessarily inhibited when we assume that a social front – a construct marked by a blend of seriousness, optimism, stiffness and fakery – is the truth about what other humans are actually like; when we side with the outward presentation of others over what we know of ourselves, namely, that we are within our depths all highly vulnerable, silly, funny, weird, desperate and sad creatures longing for affection and never far from chaos.

We cease to be warm or authentic when we double down on efforts to fit in with a model of decorum to which we see others subscribing. We get locked into interactions in which everyone's presentational self is taken by others to be the truth of who they are. Everyone lies and, even worse, everyone gets taken in by everyone else's lies – and eventually even their own.

Often, no one is having a good time in their relationships – and yet somehow everyone colludes to suggest that there might be such a thing as happy love. Everyone is miserable at work and yet everyone is busy sharing stories of their latest triumphs and progress, and thereby denying public recognition of the universal compromises and pains of careers. Everyone is breaking down in tears and crying wildly into their pillows at night, and yet still the chatter is about options for happiness and success. In a more minor key, everyone is sitting down for a tedious three-course meal when, in reality, it would be so much more fun to cook some scrambled eggs and go dancing.

The person who founders in friendship goes along with the lies. They assume that what they feel has no echo in others. They imagine that other people inside are the way they come across outside. They don't keep faith that these companions have just fallen into a straightjacketed way of living and are longing to be released, if only they knew how.

On the other hand, the bold acquaintance, the person with a natural manner and a gift for friendship, uses themselves as a guide to social reality and conduct. They know that they are bored at the dinner party – and dare to guess that on this basis many other people will be too. They know that the prize-winning novel was pretentious and they have the wherewithal to assume that they won't be the only ones to feel this way. They operate with the idea that most of what is going on in them will, despite an absence of immediate evidence, be going on inside other people too. They know they cannot be the exceptions; they refuse to trust – where it counts – in their own originality. They know that their madness and silliness, playfulness and impatience belong to everyone.

Their honesty can lend them a gift for comedy. They smoke out others' secrets when declaring their truths – and generate relieved laughter in the process. They say that they fancy the president or the shopkeeper and everyone giggles because their own unacknowledged desires have been tickled along the way. They express hatred for a fashionable political cause – and allow everyone to admit that they have long felt this way too.

Like a shy person, a socially liberated one knows they are odd. Where the latter differs is in being sure that everyone else is as well. The art of making friends is based on a sure sense that others are not as alien as they might seem; on losing some of our shame and more boldly picturing that our unusual-sounding insides have corollaries in strangers; on accepting that we are, in the best and most redemptive of ways, far from unique.

4. The fear of having nothing interesting to say

We are often held back in social life by a feeling that we can have nothing very interesting to say – chiefly because nothing especially dramatic ever happens to us. We may have a quite ordinary job; we seldom travel; the outward circumstances of our lives are settled. On this basis, we can end up assuming that we won't especially be able to intrigue or delight anyone, and so we may fall rapidly silent in interactions.

What this unfortunate line misses is that there is no such thing as a boring life, only a life that has been unfairly interpreted and narrated, perhaps by its owner. The clearest evidence for this is the extent to which some of the greatest works of art – they might be paintings and novels, films or comedy shows – are woven out of everyday, undramatic cloth. They involve nothing grander than ordinary men and women stumbling through daily realities – but these become promptly fascinating (funny or intellectually deep, beautiful or moving) because they have been presented to us with special receptivity and insight. The works of Vermeer and Jane Austen, Larry David and Marcel Proust, Virginia Woolf and Lady Murasaki (to cite just a few examples) are resolutely fashioned out of so-called 'ordinary material'. There are no great military exploits; no one is especially distinguished or legendary;

nothing much 'happens'. And yet the works of art that result are some of the most compelling that have ever been made – proof that what makes a life gripping is not so much what objectively occurs in it as the way in which it is explored and told. The most seemingly ordinary event – a daydream at the window, an interaction with a child, a walk in the park – can become a topic of hilarity or majesty when it is handled with due respect and imagination. Our lives are already as interesting as we ever need them to be, so long as we can accurately honour their true contents.

The American essayist Ralph Waldo Emerson once remarked: 'In the minds of geniuses, we find – once more – our own neglected thoughts.' In other words, geniuses don't have thoughts that are in the end so very different from our own; they have simply had the confidence to take them more seriously. Rather than imagining that their minds are only a pale shadow of the minds of infinitely greater thinkers who lived and died elsewhere long ago, they have been respectful enough of their existence to conceive that one or two properly valuable or vivid ideas might plausibly choose to alight in the familiar aviary of their own intelligences. Thinking is – in a way we generally refuse to imagine – a truly democratic activity. We all have very similar and very able minds; where so-called 'interesting' people differ is in their more confident inclinations to study them properly.

Every life – our own included – is, properly understood, immensely complex and moving. We read, we think, we observe, we have an intricate emotional history; we love and hate and hope and fear. It cannot be true that we are essentially uninteresting. We only ever unfairly lose faith in our inalienable capacity to interest others.

5. The belief in simplicity

One of the saving graces of relationships is that they are broadly understood to be very complicated things indeed. People appreciate that couples will constantly end up locked in disputes and tensions over apparently innocuous things – and may then need to spend an inordinate amount of time working their way through their differences, perhaps with the help of a psychotherapist or a mediator. It doesn't surprise anyone when a couple has a major stand-off because of the way one of them does (or doesn't do) the washing-up, or says the word 'please', or behaved around their aunt at supper. Wearily, we understand that living with a partner is an awesomely intricate business and – on a good day – we are willing to give this intricacy the respect and the time it requires.

Friendship, on the other hand, can find us more optimistic, less guarded – and more blithe. We assume that, here, things will at last be relatively easy, largely on the basis that – quite often, for a while – they indeed are. Friendships are meant to be the generous, kind and fun part of life. We come here with an expectation of ease and emotionally unburdened interactions. Not for friends the ponderous self-absorption and obsessiveness that we know from couples.

Except – of course – it rarely works out entirely this way, paradoxically, especially in those friendships that are particularly valuable and worth preserving. The more a friendship deepens, the more likely we are to stumble upon many of the same issues that complicate relationships. But here, unlike in love, we are bereft of an ideology that can render us appropriately patient and respectful of the shoals we've hit. We're fatefully convinced that we need to be breezy and light precisely where – now – we should allow ourselves to be cautious, compassionate and committed to painstaking exploration. We wind up torn between an impulse to have our case heard and an impression that we surely shouldn't be so 'heavy' in this arena.

We should not make our lives more complicated than they need to be by insisting on an illusory simplicity. The human mind is one of the most sensitive – and easily bruised – organs in the cosmos. In the course of our social lives, however serious and apparently dignified we are, we are likely to be impacted by some of the following:

- A friend who, at the end of messages, is uninclined to end matters with the 'xx' we privately expect and always give them.

- A friend who never asks about our health, though we always remember to address the kidney issue or backache they mentioned to us last year.

- A friend who insists on meeting on Tuesdays though they know that Thursdays are marginally easier for us.

- A friend who keeps alluding – in a quiet but significant way – to the wealth differential between us.

Our belief in the 'ease' of friendship contains a hidden fragility: unlike in love, we feel we are not allowed to scream across the room and tell a friend they've betrayed us. We can't, like an ardent partner, say that we hate them right now and want out. We can't – most significantly of all – dissolve our frustrations in generous and passionate acts of love-making.

In the worst case, we end up having to walk away from someone we are fond of because we're unable to tell them that – for a time at least, in order subsequently to recover sincere affection – we need to hate them quite a lot. The alluring idea that friends should never criticise one another ends up undermining the very friendships we most value.

We need to remove the pressure on individual friendships to be devoid of tensions. We should conduct all our friendships under a general, socially endorsed notion that – naturally – the more we get to know someone, the more issues will crop up. The more there will be resentments and points of contention and the more we will need to rely on artificial-sounding resolution mechanisms to dispel grievances without either side being made to feel that something has gone irrevocably wrong.

One suggestion is that – without anything significant being understood by this – good friends should regularly air between them the question: 'Tell me, what have I recently done to annoy you?' Significantly, the enquiry shouldn't probe whether or not one has annoyed the friend; the starting assumption – far less pejoratively – is that naturally one has done so (because every good friend does) and one simply needs to know the details.

With good cheer and an absence of paranoia or despair, one might point out to a friend that one was a little irked by a recent email; the friend might then respond by recounting a sensitivity raised by one's attitude to time-keeping or to boasting about one's promotion. Each person would welcome a complaint as evidence that their friend was taking their connection seriously; an inability to come up with any offence might seem like a sign that one was either being dishonestly sentimental or didn't like one's friend enough to acknowledge their power to perturb one.

We start to properly value our friendships when we grant that they are often every bit as tricky – and every bit as worthy of being rescued through analysis and discussion – as our most meaningful love stories.

6. Envy

Friendships that begin harmoniously when two people are at similar points in life are always vulnerable to the pressures of diverging fortunes: someone's novel takes off; a business booms; a promotion is proffered. Or, conversely: a career flatlines; there's a redundancy; a scandal breaks. The success of the one then becomes intensely resented by the other, who cannot look on their formerly equal friend's new advantages without contortions of sickness. Far more than we're usually prepared to admit, all friendships are at risk of envy.

In strongly individualistic and competitive societies, this can feel like a tragic truth. The highly successful and socially well-connected American essayist Gore Vidal once summarised the problem with legendary arch emphasis: 'Whenever a friend of mine succeeds, a small part of me dies.' The bleakness comes down to statistics: because the chances of one friend growing more successful over time than the other in some way must be close to 100%, all friendships are – in this disenchanted world-view – condemned gradually to wither.

The challenges are real, but they are not beyond thought or remedy. Firstly, we should never compound matters by assuming that envy might not exist, or wonder for too long whether we're imagining that it might have arisen. Those silences, missing questions and distant looks mean exactly what we suspect they do. We shouldn't presume that any bond might be without at least an important degree of this ubiquitous feeling.

And the reasons are self-evident. We tend to be friends with people who share our aspirations and values, and it is therefore highly likely that at some point along our journey together, either they will acquire something we very much want, or vice versa: it might be a partner, a profession, a qualification or a home. But it will be something for sure. We envy people for the same reason we are friends with them: because we like the same sorts of things.

We are unhelpfully inclined to be sentimental and therefore dishonest on this score: we deny that we could possibly harbour envy for someone we also like, which can lead us to unconvincing denials and cuts off opportunities for processing and growth. We need to learn to feel better about envy, in order not to have to twist our characters to avoid admitting to it.

We should, with reasonable good cheer, simply own up to our envy as we would to a sore knee or an ulcer. Children can be good guides in this area: an average 4-year-old is comedically open about their ravenous jealousy. They don't contort themselves into knots in the name of politeness. They wail immediately when their friend gets a better fire truck – or try to hit them over the head or gouge out their eyes. Parents tend to be so shocked by this that they force the child into fruitless denials. They inspire them to hide their envy from two people: the person they're envious of and, far worse, from themselves. They implicitly teach their offspring a pernicious and untrue idea: that you cannot both be a nice person and envy something your friend has. And therefore, tragically, in adult friendships, neither party is left able to call out the problem sensibly or deal with it maturely, leaving it to fester in embarrassment instead.

This brings us to the second solution to envy in friendships: we should go in for mutual playful, non-pejorative moments of confession. All good friends should – in an entirely good-natured way – routinely discuss the presence of envy between them. The question shouldn't be whether or not there is envy, just what sort of envy it might be this week. Friends should, for example, over dinner each write on a sheet of paper: 'What I am envious of now ...' and laugh with great compassion at the results.

An important part of the reason why we don't process envy as we might is that we imagine there can be only one solution to the emotion: that the person who has something that their friend lacks will have to hand it over. But of course, we can't be expected to surrender our partner, our house or our position nearer the top of the company to make a friend feel better. However, that's not remotely necessary, because what the person who envies us really wants is not, in the end, our love life or accommodation or profession. What they want is reassurance. They want to know that we still love them despite our new advantages. They crave to be told that though we have won the lottery, sold our shares or found a dazzling lover, we remain deeply attached to them and care for them as much as we ever did.

Deep down, the pain of rivalry masks a fear of abandonment. When we are in the weaker position, our terror is that the other – in the glory of their new success – will stop caring about us. They'll start to pity us, to look down on us and to want to shake us off. We're no longer worthy in their eyes (we imagine) of close association with them. These are genuinely horrifying thoughts. But it's crucial, at this moment of fear, to ask ourselves how we would feel about them if the situation were reversed. Suppose we ended up with a lot more money or prestige than them; would we relish making them feel hopeless? Would we want to crush them? On the contrary, we'd be rather desperate to make sure our friend knew as securely as possible that we saw them just as we always did, that we loved them for reasons that were unaffected by promotions or money. We then need to remember that if this is true of us, it will also be true of our friend. One person may have made a fortune by launching a business, the other may subsist on busking (let's imagine), but between the two money is not the mark of worth; it is, as it always was, their conversations about books, childhood, the complexity of being alive, their responsiveness to nature and art, their sense of humour. True friends don't take their cues from what others may think. They evaluate (and deeply respect) each other on a different – and far better – scale of values than that crudely utilised by markets and employers.

Another major defence that protects friendship from being eaten alive by rivalry is – oddly – pride. To feel the force of this idea we need to abstract, for a moment, from the particular relationship in which rivalry is rearing its head and think about our wider attitude to relationships. Suppose one day someone who is very impressive and successful were to get interested in us and extend an open and benign hand of friendship. We'd be deeply proud to count them amongst our closest companions. We'd relish that despite all the demands from the wider world and the great opportunities that constantly came their way, they wanted to talk and spend time with us; they wanted and valued our views and ideas; they liked and greatly appreciated who we were. This wouldn't be humiliating; it would be wonderful. At root, this is no different from continuing to be a close friend to someone who achieves conspicuous success during the time of our acquaintanceship. We deserve to be proud of them, and – importantly – proud of ourselves for being friends with them.

Owning up to our true longing (and hearing it appeased) is devilishly hard for reasons we're now in a position to appreciate: because the envious person can't admit to what they're feeling; because there aren't generally any good occasions on which confessions can be made – and because we aren't collectively schooled in the art of offering reassurance to others in the wake of our successes.

In a better world, we would take greater care. As a matter of course, every time something went well for us, we would be sure to add in ample reassurance that – despite our new status – we continued to love and cherish those we had long loved. We should stop worrying that there might be seams of envy entangled in our friendships and focus instead on a far more important goal: learning to handle envy with kindness, honesty and well-apportioned doses of warmth and humour.

7. The difficulty of imagining the loneliness of others

One of the reasons why we tend not to make friends as often as we might comes down to a powerful background idea whose full destructive force we may not even be aware of: *the belief that any decent person already has all the friends they need.*

Somewhere in our minds, the notion has been lodged that only very sad and inept people would – at this stage in their lives (whatever stage one happens to be at) – still have a space in their social agenda for a new entrant. Everyone else – anyone worth knowing, anyone talented, interesting and good – would long ago have acquired the gang to which they are now continuously and irredeemably wedded.

What this idea misses is the extent to which loneliness and disenchantment are ongoing and universal possibilities, and not limited to those of reduced appeal and capacities. Right now, the enchanting actor is (despite the crowds) lonely, as is the feted concert pianist, the renowned biologist, the skilled airline pilot, the miraculous neurosurgeon and that rather nice-looking person you have just spotted in the corner of the room laughing animatedly with a group of fashionable companions.

Anyone of sensitivity and charm might fail to find the right sort of allies, outgrow their friends from school or university, land on uncongenial spirits at work and spend a lot of evenings on their own, either physically or spiritually. And we can know this for certain of other people because we know it, first and foremost, from a very reliable source: ourselves.

We need to battle the part of our minds that reads our isolation as a selective punishment and vanquish it with evidence available directly from our own experience. Other people who know us almost certainly find it hard to imagine that we are lonely and that we'd like to locate a wise, tender, funny and interesting new friend, and it's statistically improbable that we would be outliers in this respect. What holds true for us must and will hold true for others.

We have built a predominantly cold and guarded society by imagining a thesis that we know to be untrue on the basis of our own experience. We have allowed self-hatred and shame to cloud our judgement and reduce what is in fact a universal affliction and possibility to the status of a personal curse.

The next time we spot an interesting person, we should disregard our initial assumption that they have all the friends they need. We don't have exactly the right people in our circle –

and neither, most probably, do they. We can afford to shed our false background thesis of social existence and go and say hello.

8. Too many friends

One of the more unexpected reasons why a person may end up not having any friends is, paradoxically, because they have far too many already.

As friend-abundant people, we may seem like the last people to suffer from feelings of abandonment and forlornness. We might be invited out all the time; there may have been 23 people at our recent birthday party and there might be 123 of them attending our forthcoming wedding. Our phones might constantly buzz with new messages and we may not have been home for an evening on our own for two months. We don't seem like candidates for loneliness. And yet, this is precisely what we could be, not because no one knows us but because *everyone* knows us. We have been surreptitiously driven to loneliness not by an absence of friends but by a crippling and ongoing plethora of them. We are lonely not because we are alone but because company has stripped us of opportunities for the sort of focused intimacy required to dissolve the more stubborn roots of isolation.

We have ended up in this confusing space in part because of an ambiguity in our societal understanding of what a 'friend' might be. At a popular level, the term seems to refer to someone we catch up with once or twice a year, whose job and relationship we vaguely understand, around whose arm we often place our own and whom we greet with great affection and a momentary longing for sincerity at large social gatherings where music makes it hard to speak.

But at another level, the word 'friend' also refers to someone who is never more than a phone call away, someone we spoke to this morning and whom we'll be in touch with again at lunchtime and then once more again before evening, someone who understands us as well as a lover or a parent, someone whom we adore as much as a sibling, someone who would be there at our hospital bed at the end and for whom we would – *in extremis* – be ready to lay down our lives.

It's a failure of language that both these sorts of people blithely carry the same title – but the confusion is more than linguistic. It causes us in practice to forget what we might best do with those we like.

We might assert – in sharp contradiction to the messages of society – that it is impossible to have many more than three proper friends. Four would be a maximum. At five, something has gone wrong. And by the time we invite over a hundred people to our wedding or can fill a restaurant for a birthday (even a landmark one), we have traduced the concept of friendship entirely.

Reasons that go beyond the financial or the physical explain why people tend not to have more than a few children. It appears impossible to maintain the sort of close emotional bonds that both parties crave once the numbers rise. We know that someone could not possibly be honouring the role of father or mother if they had obligations across twenty people. But a similar modesty escapes us when it comes to friendship, where we can imagine that it might be possible to be a friend worthy of the word to a group that could fill a tennis court.

In reality, proper friendships require time and close attention. We need to continually check in on those we profess to love; we have to keep their stories in mind; we need the emotional bandwidth to receive their sorrows and excitements and to maintain a sincerity born out of novelty in our disclosures and responses.

To have any friends, we may therefore need to do something that could sound odd and even rather mean (but isn't either of these things): fire most of our existing friends. We may need to choose intensity over breadth. This hints at why many of us may find the move rather hard. True friendship requires commitment – which also necessarily entails emotional risk.

Once we start to love our friends, rather than merely consort with a stadium full of them, dangers start to mount. We might be abandoned; if a best friend stopped liking us, we might suffer an agony as great as any break-up. We rediscover in relation to true friendship some of the same attachment fears that bedevil us in love. But now at least we can know what is at play: we aren't hanging out with a group because we are fulfilled, but because we are – at heart – terrified of the risks implied in more focused commitment.

We need to become specialists of friendship rather than its unwittingly isolated and forlorn generalists. People new to the idea of friendship may have a great many friends; those who have begun to understand what the institution can deliver have learnt to count them on a few fingers of one hand.

III.

Friends of Friendship

One of civilisation's main ambitions is to help us turn what might seem like lucky accidents into regular and repeatable experiences. We see this in agriculture, which seeks to produce regular supplies of the sorts of foods that our earliest ancestors would have viewed as unique and rare blessings. What was once a lone berry bush will make way for a whole field of cultivated crops. But civilisation, with its powers of reasoning, logic and organisation, does not need to limit itself to the production of material goods. It might – wielded correctly – be the instrument that helps us to acquire psychological nutrients too, including those of friendship. Often we still think of a good friendship as a lucky accident. We imagine that we alight on a great friend with some of the happenstance of stumbling on a succulent fruit tree. We don't think that we can plot to make friends as we might plot to grow strawberries or harvest apricots. But such modesty is not grounded in truth. We could set out to crack the code of friendship as we would the puzzle of plant biology. We can go in search of the constituents of successful friendship and systematically identify the friends of friendship.

1. Good listening

History is filled with people who grew famous for being good at speaking. However, there is no comparably glorious roster of those who have been acclaimed for doing something equally or even arguably more valuable: listening properly. Our collective idea of participating in conversation has from the first been unfairly focused on what people manage to say, almost never on what they manage to *hear.*

In a world where everyone seems to talk past one another, to genuinely listen is one of the most constructive and warm-hearted things we can ever offer another person – and a major building block of any worthwhile union. Friendship is the dividend of gratitude we are likely to want to offer a companion who can put aside their concerns and make our own turmoils vivid and clear in their minds for a time.

Crucially, we do not – most of us – set out to be such poor listeners. We are so only by accident and for rather poignant reasons too: because no one has ever properly listened to us. We are trapped within a vortex of mutual disregard that makes every individual less likely to know how to appease another's yearnings. What then might be some of the key moves that a good listener could make in order to reverse the collective slide towards universal deafness?

The first is to get better at offering encouragement to those who speak to us. Contrary to expectations, most of us do not naturally have a torrent of things we feel we want to tell others. Years of not being listened to take their toll. We easily feel we are boring; we have been hammered into assuming that our voices are not especially compelling and that our reflections do not merit sustained attention. We're therefore likely to start a story with a certain hesitation and then, looking around us furtively, to stop at the slightest hint of tedium. 'Oh it doesn't really matter,' we might say, before turning a friend's focus elsewhere. When we come close to something especially raw and fascinating, remembering how often such material hasn't landed properly, we may be beset by an acute impression of offending those around us. 'You can't possibly find this interesting,' we may insist, just as we approach a truly important detail that we long in our depths to be understood for.

An early task of a good listener, therefore, is to help quash the speaker's self-doubt. When they feel their friend stumbling or losing confidence, good listeners will be ready with a swift and heartfelt 'That's so interesting' or a sympathetic and highly attuned 'Go on ...'

Shaped by unreceptive histories, speakers tend to rush over their accounts: 'It was a difficult childhood, I suppose ...'; 'Mum was often unwell at that time ...'; 'Dad can be a bit elsewhere when he drinks ...' The good listener intimates how much more must lie beneath these summaries and is ready with follow-up questions: 'How did it make you feel?'; 'Were there particular incidents that stuck out?'; 'What was the house like at that time?' These second-order enquiries, however slight, provide the crucial, and so often absent, signal that tells the speaker: 'I am here, I am engaged, and I want to understand more.' Such curiosity has a transformative effect. In the right company, we start to feel more interesting to ourselves on the basis that we have managed to animate someone else. A pleasant friend is someone who says interesting things to us. A really great one does something yet more valuable: helps us to find ourselves interesting.

The single best way to show that we have properly heard someone is to repeat what they have said using slightly different words. They might, for example, tell us: 'Mum and Dad were keen to suggest that everything was fine, but we children knew it wasn't true. What's more, the constant cheerfulness started to weigh on us because we suspected it was a sign of trouble ...' The good listener scans the narrative and carefully repackages it in alternative but faithful language: 'So it seems you were living with a lot of lies and began to distrust the good times ...' With a well-formed précis, we aren't just told that someone has heard us; we have visceral proof that they have done so.

As they pay attention to a speaker, a good listener will become aware of how often painful and difficult material is imparted without the layer of emotions that it rightly deserves. Stories of divorce, illness, death or poverty may be narrated in a factual way without exploring their psychological impact. This is another legacy of having lived in a depleted environment without being encouraged to acknowledge what it felt like. The good listener helps to return a raft of missing feelings to the speaker – be they of anger or loss, grief or melancholy. 'That sounds really tough,' the listener might say. Or: 'That must have hurt a lot.' Or simply, with warm, sad eyes: 'I'm so sorry.' A story that might have been told entirely without affect suddenly starts to move the speaker themselves. They can – perhaps for the first time – directly experience the emotions that the prevailing inattention had denied them. There may be many tears.

In all this, there is one important move that good listeners *don't* attempt: they don't – however seductive it might appear – make any direct bid to solve the speaker's problems. They step sharply back from what – at first sight – may seem like an obvious and kindly act: to reassure a friend and solve their difficulties.

They don't tell those worried about their employment that the dispute at work is sure to have a happy ending. They don't give practical advice about how to find a better partner. They don't rush to deliver a lecture on why a Stoic approach to pain always reaps dividends. They do something infinitely wiser and kinder: they let the speaker explore their own feelings of confusion and distress without a panicky urge to force a neatly packaged resolution on them. They don't allow their own anxieties around sharing pain to stifle their companion's chance to express themselves.

It's easy to grow vague about what friendship – and the love that underpins it – might really involve. We will know we have found a friend worthy of the word when we feel patiently and quietly witnessed in our entirety, in all our painful and chaotic complexity. Friends sometimes ask one another what they might want for their birthdays. There is only one answer worth giving, a luxury and a privilege so great we may have lost sight of how much we long for it: to be properly listened to for an hour or so.

2. Setting an agenda

The word 'agenda' is not normally one we associate with 'friendship'. The thought that a friend might have one can quickly come across as an incongruously mercenary and cynical possibility. We tend to connect agendas with attempts to increase status, raise money, steal an advantage or hoodwink others. We tend to like our friendships to be very much agenda-free.

Even asking what a friendship might be 'for' can seem odd. In an otherwise overly reductive world, we view friendship as offering a last hold-out against practical and commercial pressures. If asked, we might, with irritation, simply say that we want our friendships to be 'for' not very much – beyond providing that nebulous but crucial quality we know as 'friendliness'.

But in our haste to escape from reductiveness, we risk drifting away from the ultimate purpose of a friendship. Whether we are conscious of it or not, friendships generally do (and should) have agendas, and the more we can get these in view, the more we can be in a position to assess a given friendship's significance and role. It doesn't have to contravene the ideals of friendship to occasionally ask what we are essentially trying to do with any friend we spend time with. 'Do' doesn't have to involve a material or competitive move; we might be alluding to a mission to offer reassurance about backache or an exchange of views on 1970s electric guitar solos. The question doesn't have to shatter what is precious in a friendship; it may just help us to hold it more securely in mind.

We can start from the fundamental idea that we need friends because we can't carry out certain things – ranging from the practical to the emotional – on our own. Friendship is born out of our insufficiencies. Yet what we lack will sharply differ from person to person (and age to age). Some of us aren't good at laughing at ourselves; others need help in adopting a more reasonable perspective; some of us need assistance in being more forgiving; others require help in growing more ruthless. Equally, there are areas in which we're likely already to excel. We may be world masters at the art of fretting, or of worrying about our status, or of believing that everything is fine as it is.

The nature of the things we can't do well alone should end up determining the sorts of friends that we would – ideally – set out to have in our lives (and conversely, the sorts of people we probably shouldn't surround ourselves with). The agenda for our friendships should be set by our deficiencies; there are as many of these potential agendas as there are gaps in our psyches.

We could, in theory, spend an evening talking about almost anything with a nice person: we could shift – pleasantly enough – from what happened at work last week to where we're planning to go on holiday to a film we happened to see the night before. We could proceed as if we had endless time and unlimited energy. But the drive to ask for an agenda is founded on a stern but vital insight: we have a bounded lifespan. And on that basis, we owe it to ourselves and our companions to work hard to zero in on the most important, thrilling, heart-warming or fruitful activities we could plausibly carry out with a particular person.

In one kind of friendship, a common agenda might involve trying to clarify one's priorities in the last phase of one's life: how much does money still matter? When might one retire? How much energy should one give to the children? Another friendship might be focused on understanding one's relationships, or the art of Northern India, or the best way to exercise or to plant a garden. It is no injustice to the sincerity of a bond to be as clear as we can about why it exists.

The concept of an agenda also helps along the way to explain why at times we fail to click with someone as we might. It isn't so much that we don't like them; it can simply be that we can't – in the deepest of senses – find any use for them. There is nothing they can give us that we lack and vice versa. We properly honour friendship when we accept that every friend we truly value should by rights be playing a significant role in advancing us towards the overarching goal of every life: growing into the most mature, articulate, developed and expansive version of oneself.

3. Acts of service

Our time on earth may be far less enjoyable than it should be because of an unfortunate and peculiar idea that has taken hold of our collective thinking: that the ultimate purpose of life is to make ourselves as happy as possible. Encouraged by this now-dominant concept, we're goaded to try to make as much money as we can, to spend it lavishly on costly and rare goods, to divert ourselves with a plethora of entertainments and distractions and to get others to cater to all of our wishes and whims.

It's a seductive vision, but the more precise and surprising psychological truth is that human satisfaction has an overwhelmingly different source: it derives from a feeling of being needed by other people. We grow at peace with ourselves the more we can either alleviate the suffering or increase the delight of someone else. We are hard-wired to seek to make a difference even as we are, most of us, structurally hopeless at making ourselves content for more than fifteen minutes. Our characters can be relied upon to pull against any attempts at hedonic maximisation. Our psychological complexities have a habit of trailing us into the fanciest, most apparently desirable places. We have bitter arguments in the marble hallways of luxury hotels, despair descends on exotic paradise islands, melancholy hovers over poolside bars, and in the midst of a costly spa day we may be gripped by lassitude and irritation – and long to return home to bed and cry.

But we may, with time, come to a deeply relieving alternative realisation: that the route to satisfaction lies in pushing thoughts of ourselves aside for a while in the name of trying to help others. Joy comes from acts of service. We may personally be lost causes, but others – with needs that are perhaps easier or more urgent than our own – offer us opportunities to exercise our talents and flex our capacities.

We developed over thousands of generations to serve our tribes: we found the food or pounded the grain; we kept watch at night to keep others safe; we made decisions on which everyone's survival depended. Any prestige we had was the result of the good we accomplished for others. This is where our pride, our sense of accomplishment and our self-respect have their roots. But in the febrile conditions of modernity, our instinct to contribute effectively to others' lives has largely been dissipated and lost. Such is the nature of the economy; our jobs seldom give us any direct sense of being of use to anyone. The gap between worker and customer has grown immense and tangled. We might be occupied day to day by making sure a company we don't especially admire ships tiny parts for engines used to make Jacuzzis bubble, or protects insurance firms from litigation when they have reneged on their full promises after winter storms. Or we're paid well to market casino tickets or beer-hall memberships to an audience that should rightly be diverting its money elsewhere. We may be doing fine by the conventions of our age, but what we've been denied is any sense that our intelligence has been angled towards anything remotely honourable.

Until, that is, we receive news that a friend is unwell. We might have wanted to go and see a film or have a massage; we could have been weighing up whether to get a haircut or invest in a wine cellar. But a far greater opportunity is at hand. We are no surgeon and our powers of restoration are limited. Nevertheless, we can finally do something important. We can make a large batch of chicken soup (with plentiful onions and carrots) and ladle it into easy-to-open containers, each of which we mark clearly for a particular day of the week. We can gather berries and chocolate, fresh bread and a bag of cereal. We may have failed at a lot already; we might be on our second marriage and not be on great terms with our children. But we now have a role and a right to exist because we are proving incalculably important to someone who is recently home from keyhole heart surgery and finds it difficult to make it down the stairs unaided.

The good news is that once we properly realise that we can make a difference to others, our room for action opens up in unlimited ways. The sick are everywhere, as are the lonely, the heartbroken, the sad, the spiritually exhausted and those with cardiac conditions.

It can be sweet when a friend thanks us profusely for being nice to them, as if we'd done something that deserved special praise. The truth is that we enjoyed, far more than we can admit, the chance to be overtly, clearly and effectively good. The friend who needed us provided us with an opportunity to know that our lives are not in fact wholly superfluous, that we are not monsters of disappointment and grumpiness, that we aren't always as clumsy as we are in relationships or as grandiose or prickly as we can come across at work. We do, in fact, still have the power to be decent and effective human beings. More rightly viewed, the thanks should be going entirely the other way.

4. Better questions

One of the most common but also unusually difficult questions we are liable to face in any long-term friendship, especially at the start of every new encounter, is: 'What have you been up to recently?'

We meet up with a friend we haven't seen in a while and – fair enough – they want to know what has been happening to us since we last saw them, and we, similarly, want to know the same about them. The mystery of individual existence is at play; two people are on a quest to break through the barriers of isolation and commune around a rich understanding of one another's recent travails, fears and joys.

But there's a problem. If our lives are in any way typical, we won't – of course – have been up to anything that feels remotely noteworthy. We haven't gone anywhere special; no one has died; we haven't been sent on any remote or challenging missions; there hasn't been any particular intrigue or significant professional development. With a degree of weariness and shame, we may once more simply have to brush away the question with an 'Oh, not so much really'.

The more poignant reality, however, is that quite a lot has been happening. It always does. But it has been doing so at a subatomic level, at the level of emotional and perceptual change, which the enquiry, like a butterfly net with the wrong mesh size, is not well suited to catch. We may not have been involved in any outward dramas, but we have – deep in ourselves – felt a stream of sensations and ideas, as evanescent and fragile as they are significant and suggestive. Really quite a lot has been going on; it's just that the question we are responding to doesn't help us to make sense of any of it.

We deserve – and here societal conventions are predominantly to blame – to be on the receiving end of better sorts of question. In order to catch the marrow of life and to more accurately track the movements of another's soul, we should normalise the raising and answering of new questions that skilfully pick up on the precise, detailed, intimate, sensory and, in the best ways, odd-sounding aspects of existence. We might, in a better-arranged world, learn to make use of some of the following:

- Have you rubbed your fingertips along any interesting materials recently?
- What images have been in your mind as you've been falling asleep?

- Are there particular bits of your past you've been feeling close to lately?
- What regrets have emerged?
- Who do you want to apologise to?
- What interesting or moving things have you spotted on your commute to and from work?
- What adjectives might capture the mood of this stretch of your life?
- What would the 5-year-old you think about who you are at the moment?
- In an ideal love affair that you'd like to have now, what might happen? Where would you want to be? What would you be doing for one another? What would they understand about you?
- What items from your wardrobe are you wearing most at this time?
- What is sad right now?
- What positions have you been sleeping in?
- What smells define this period of time? And what colours?
- What do you want to find out more about? What would you want explained to you? What sort of book would be really appropriate to read right now?
- What emotional puzzles are you – in the background – wrestling with?

- Where do you feel misunderstood?
- What are you impatient for?
- If this period of time was a shape, it might be a ...? And a sound ...? And a taste ...? And a sort of jam or condiment ...?

What we end up seeing in the world and in ourselves depends on the implicit questions we carry in us – which in turn reflect the sort of questions we have most often been asked by others. The more acute the questions we are asked, the more we will take note of.

One of the ways to think of certain works of art is as distinctive answers to fine-grained enquiries about what has been going on in someone's life. If we had, for example, met the mid-century Italian painter Giorgio Morandi at a dinner party and asked him what he'd been up to recently, he might have struggled to come up with the sort of anecdotal material expected in a reply. But in the medium of his art, we find an exquisitely detailed record of what was truly going on for him and might, in a general way, be going on for us too. His paintings – many of which were painted in World War II during fierce Allied bombing in his native Bologna – contain no accounts of anything that could count as newsworthy. But they nevertheless deftly sensitise us to the movements of another's soul. We see a succession of

Giorgio Morandi, *Still Life*, 1946

well-arranged vases, glasses and bottles, bathed in a variety of diffuse morning and evening lights. Morandi seems to be telling us: 'And this is life too. This is what we see when we rightly understand what an occurrence is.' His art symbolises a protest against an overly materially based interpretation of eventfulness. A truly significant happening might simply be that at 5.30 p.m., a shaft of light struck the stem of a vase and created an impression of harmony and repose. Or that at dawn, a bowl on the sideboard acquired a creamy texture that evoked the mystery of early childhood. This is reality as well, Morandi is hinting, once we learn to catch it with the right instrument.

Though we may not be turning out any paintings, we are all – in our minds, in a latent way – as observant, emotionally rich and easily impacted as any artist. The reason for our normal social muteness is that, through no fault of our own, we haven't been given the opportunity to divulge what is at play within us. By expecting to sum up our lives as a series of events, we miss what they are in fact made up of – a discreet tapestry of sense impressions, longings, griefs, daydreams and easily erased intimations of beauty and pain.

So much has been happening to us of late. We're just waiting for attentive friends to help us catch some of it with the right questions.

5. Confessions

Our friendships are so much poorer than they might be because of a regrettable belief that, in order to be worthy of affection, we should do everything to appear 'normal' to those closest to us.

In the name of this ideal, we make strenuous attempts to wash away the reality of our complicated and wayward natures. We suggest that we are far simpler than we are. We strive to erase our compulsions and our sinfulness, our perversion and our innocence, our rage and our tenderness. We clean ourselves up to greet our circle and along the way destroy opportunities to commune around our wretched and difficult truths.

The highest purpose of friendship lies in a capacity to offer a fellow broken human a hopeful and redemptive message: *I – like you – have been odd; I – like you – have been mad; I – like you – have been guilty. No one is normal, and therefore no one is beyond love and sympathy.*

But how seldom we venture such candour. Let's imagine that you and your partner have been getting on increasingly badly. It happens all the time (though still we greet our domestic problems as if they were isolated curses rather than universal afflictions). You tried to get a point across. They held an opposing line. You thought you were making progress; they seemed – in your eyes – to be holding things up vindictively and unreasonably. And then, after three and a half hours of talking, it happened: the apparently very strange, very abnormal, very unusual move that seems to place you beyond the circle of understanding. You called them an idiot; they called you a shithead. You went into the bathroom and, starting from the thumb end, put the palm of your hand deep in your mouth and bit very hard, so hard that there was blood and there are still teeth marks to this day.

We tell ourselves that friendship is an arena in which we can share our troubles with a fellow interested and sympathetic soul. But we also strongly suspect that mutual support in friendship is governed by an unstated rule: that our problems can never be very serious. Unfortunate things happen, of course, but they are to be quickly brushed away with a joke and a few heartening words. There are bumps on the road, but we must – to assure the union – remain essentially steady.

By the standards of polite society, hand-biting is a grotesque episode: to get so enraged is viewed as wrong in itself. How can we ever share such a thing with a friend, along with all the many other odd things we have done and will continue to do: slamming a door so hard it nearly came off its hinges; locking ourselves in the car and sobbing for an hour; fantasising about one of our partner's siblings ...?

It's tempting – in trying to convey our lives to a friend – to stick to generalities. We mention that we had 'an argument with our partner' or that we 'got a bit upset'. Yet if we are ever to liberate ourselves from the lies we have imprisoned ourselves in, we must come to our friendships with a more robust sense of what a human being is. We need to overcome the respectable fiction that we are not fearful, emotional, irrational creatures only a few millimetres from disaster and collapse at any point. It is only with great and benign efforts (and generally a lot of help from teachers and parents) that we ever learn to construct a more elegant, enlightened persona; that we get adept at maintaining a reasonable picture of ourselves and pretend that it is only certain other people (criminals, dictators) who fail to live up to this pleasing standard. But the darker truth is that our civilised selves sit on top of a tumultuous nature that is never more than a long argument and a bout of tiredness away.

We should dare to let more of our reality into our friendships. We are evidently not entirely respectable or balanced. We strive so hard to turn towards the light, but much of us will always lie in darkness. And yet we are – for all that – part of the human community, seeking permission to become friends of a deeper sort. It's moving when two friends show each other kindness and love; it's properly helpful when they also learn to show one another their darkness, their sins and the bite marks on their hands.

6. Horizontal conversations

At the dawn of psychoanalysis, Sigmund Freud made a remarkable discovery: that there can be an immense difference between what someone will tell you when they are sitting opposite you in a chair, looking you in the eye, and what they will tell you when they are lying flat on their back, looking at the ceiling.

Freud's goal was for his patients to be extremely honest with him, to divulge their true selves with as little inhibition as possible. For it was their self-ignorance and denial that, in his view, were the ultimate causes of their illnesses. A capacity to be honest was not merely refreshing; it might make the difference between sanity and despair.

But Freud also came to realise how much his own presence could be responsible for inhibiting his clients from reporting candidly on their dreams and fantasies. Something about seeing his face and feeling his eyes on them meant that patients were inclined to disguise their true selves, to hold back from the more embarrassing or sensitive material of their lives and to attempt to appear more 'normal' than was true, or good for them. Freud recognised just how much opposition there could be to talking in an unvarnished way about incest, cross-dressing, castration, impotence, cannibalism, anal sex or murder while sitting face to face, as one might in a Viennese café or a standard doctor's surgery. Hence his decision, taken in 1890, to shift his patients onto a couch, which has ever since become a mainstay of psychotherapeutic consulting rooms the world over.

More than we perhaps realise, seeing another person's face can discourage us from a confession: we edit our self-presentation in the light of their reactions; we hold back from accessing the properly interesting, complicated and troubling (and therefore important) parts of ourselves. This happens in consulting rooms, but it will happen just as often in that far more familiar context of the dinner party or social gathering. Here too, though we have come together ostensibly in order to be sincere and speak with honesty about our lives, we may succumb to a fear of sharing what is truly going on. Feeling eyes on us, we hold back from divulging our reality. We flinch at putting others off; we follow every twitch of their mouths and censor ourselves in line with what we imagine (often quite unfairly) to be their appetite for judgement and distaste. As a result, we may spend far longer than any of us want circling what happened on a recent holiday or how the house renovations are going, when there might be so much else we need and would like to share.

With Freud's example in mind, we should pioneer our own forms of horizontal conversation. After dessert or between courses, we might suggest that we all go and lie down somewhere on the floor. It might be on blankets or the carpet; in the kitchen or the hall. We might find it useful to switch off the lights.

It can be a strange sensation, to be stretched out in a darkened space with people – some of whom we may not yet know too well – with an open invitation to free-associate about our lives. We might all stay silent for two minutes to adjust to the situation. In those moments, we might think about the broad structure of our years: once we were babies, then toddlers. We went to school and it felt like it would go on forever. Then we started work, travelled, had relationships, made some big mistakes, were thrilled and sometimes despaired and now it's now. We'll get older and eventually – not as far away as we would like – we will die. We become newly conscious of voices, our own and those of others; we can hear so many more of the nuances when we aren't also being called to look, or constantly to ensure our own expression hasn't become gormless or bored.

In the dark, it matters a bit less what other people might think of us. We can be a bit more loyal to ourselves and in the process, while examining the light fittings in the gloom, we can do other people the ultimate social favour: that of letting them see our vulnerability and peculiarity, which can appease their own sense of oddity and loneliness.

We might broach some of the following sensitive themes:

- What I'm scared of is ...
- My childhood was tricky because ...
- At work I have difficulties around ...
- I feel lonely when ...
- I'm so ashamed that ...
- What I'd love more than anything is ...
- If only I wasn't so scared, I would ...
- If it didn't seem so selfish, I would ...
- If I couldn't fail, I would ...

By lying down in a strange way at dinner, we're not in reality drifting towards eccentricity. We're using an unusual manoeuvre in order to do something very sensible that we have aspired to do for a long time: finally tell other people what it is like to be us – and to hear individually strange but collectively deeply liberating truths from others about how they're getting on with the always-puzzling business of being alive.

7. A resistance to parties

The idea of being a friend-worthy person can be heavily associated with finding enjoyment in going to, and in all likelihood also in giving, parties. To be sociable means welcoming the idea of being in a room replete with an above-average number of other guests, many of whom will be strangers, most of whom will be holding a glass of alcohol, bantering, with lights lower than they normally would be, and music somewhat higher than required in order to catch the details of another's voice.

Parties have become synonymous with sociability because of certain underlying ideas about what true social connection might require and entail. We assume that sociability naturally springs up when lots of people are put together in a room, that it means speaking a lot and notably cheerfully about things that have been happening in our lives, that it depends on a jokey manner and – ideally – on the possession of a few entertaining anecdotes, often involving striking coincidences.

But such assumptions sidestep two sizeable objections. Firstly, true sociability – that is, a real connection between two people – is almost never built up via anything cheerful. It is the result of making ourselves vulnerable before another person, by revealing something that is broken, lost, confused, lonely and in pain within us. We build genuine connections when we dare to exchange thoughts that might leave us open to humiliation and judgement; we make real friends through sharing, in an uncensored and frank way, a little of the agony and confusion of being alive.

Secondly, true sociability requires an encouraging context. And at parties, sadly, we are generally under unhelpful pressure to appear normal, self-possessed and solid, to the extent that we cannot possibly disclose anything much of our true selves. Our default mode will be – without anything sinister being meant by this – to lie about who we are and what is sincerely going on in our lives.

This suggests that a genuinely social occasion might be rather different from what we typically envisage. We think of a 'good host' as someone who makes sure there is enough wine and, at a pinch, ensures people know each other's names. But in the profound sense, a good host is someone who creates the conditions in which strangers can start to feel safe about sharing the more authentic parts of themselves, even the sad and desperate parts.

A commitment to deep sociability might lead us to recognise that we depend on a little artful choreography to get us into the psychological zone in which connections can unfold. We might need tact and skill to share a little of what is sad within us. We need help to identify shared regrets, humiliations and feelings of despair.

Parties as they are currently structured constitute a clever ruse by a minority, perhaps only ten per cent of humanity, to persuade the rest of us that we have been provided with the social contact we crave. But, in truth, it takes an insular and misanthropic person to feel that what goes on at an average party really counts as anything like the requisite encounter with one's fellow human animal. If we have a lingering horror of parties, we should be generous towards our hunches. It doesn't mean that we don't like other people, but rather that we have too ambitious a conception of social contact to put up with what is on offer at most parties. The mark of a truly sociable person might, in many situations, simply be a strong desire to stay at home.

8. Acceptance

For a certain group amongst us, long stretches of our lives may be spent asking ourselves essentially the same question, with the same blend of frustration, despair and puzzlement: why am I so lonely? Why, in other words, do I so often find myself at odds in social groups; why can't I more easily connect with people; why do I not have more friends worthy of the name?

It's tempting – always – to jump to the darkest conclusion: because I am awful, because there is something wrong with me, because I deserve to be hated.

But the real answer is likely to be far less punitive and, in its way, far more logical. We, the isolated members of the tribe, are lonely for a very firm and forgivable reason: because we are interested in introspection, and they – the others – for all their intelligence and wit and strength of mind, are not.

They may have many hobbies and passions and lots to say about a host of things, but they are not especially interested in looking deeply inside themselves. It is not their idea of fun to think about their childhoods, to trace the links between their emotions and their actions, or to lie for a long time in a bath or a bed processing events in their interior lives. Introspection is not their thing. They haven't told us this in so many words – and they never will; they don't even realise it perhaps. We simply have to surmise that this is the case on the basis of external evidence: that we never feel we have much to say to them, even though – objectively – there might be so much to share.

It's the lack of introspection that explains why conversation with them so often gets stuck in odd places: discussing the price of train tickets, or the best way to prepare muffins, or what so-and-so from university (whom we never really knew or liked) is now doing. It explains why, when we try to nudge the conversation onto something more intimate and vulnerable, we seem somehow never to manage and end up in yet more rounds of discussion about the sports results or the new political scandal.

They aren't necessarily cold, but it can certainly seem that way because they aren't interested in communicating what is really going on in their hearts. Sometimes we can be surprised when, out of the blue, they tell us that they consider us to be a close friend.

We should accept that most of our acquaintances – however much they might, in theory, want to be friendly – do not want to do so at the cost of looking inside their own minds. And we for our part are lonely because we are operating with a notion of intimacy that is far less common than we torture ourselves by imagining. We will be blessed if we meet just one or two people in a lifetime who want to play as we do. The rest of the time, we shouldn't compound our problems by feeling lonely that we're lonely. It's painful but utterly understandable; our favourite pastime, however noble it might be, is a very unusual one indeed.

IV.

Substitutes for Friendship

Part of the reason why our solitary periods can feel especially dark is that we have a hard time thinking of them as anything other than a punishment. But once we learn to trust that there are many honourable reasons why someone could find themselves alone – that solitude doesn't in itself have to say anything negative about who we are – this liberates us to pursue better, less crushing approaches to solitude. We might – as people who are more generously reconciled to their own company – start to look with greater creativity and inventiveness at a range of substitutes for friendship.

1. Friends in the sky

For centuries, across vast swathes of the earth's surface, a predominant share of the population has thought of their best and closest friends as people who – through the eyes of strictly secular observers – don't exist.

In the third millennium BCE in Ancient Sumer, in what is now modern-day southern Iraq, one of the most popular friends one might have had was called Enki. A handsome, paternal man with a graceful face, a long beard and flowing robes, one could turn to him for advice on money, love and health, and he could be counted upon to respond with kindness, practical advice and sympathy.

In the Inca Empire, in what is now modern-day Peru, one's best friend might have been Inti, who had a profound interest in human sorrows, especially those pertaining to matters of fertility and agriculture.

In Māori and Polynesian mythology, a central best friend was called Tangaroa, a god who kept a watchful eye over the sea and the creatures that live there, whom one could talk to about navigation and fishing, weather patterns and ocean currents.

The best of friends: 'The Lusenberg Virgin'
parish church of St Ulrich, Val Gardena, Italy

And for the world's Catholics, Mary was the kindliest of friends, who was on hand for compassion and understanding, hope and intercession, motherly guidance and forgiveness.

Surveying the long history of faith-based imaginary friendships, atheists have tended to grow scornful, and even plain cross, at their fellow humans' perceived credulity and naivety. What shallowness, they have said, to turn a statue into a friend, to imagine that a pleasant-looking woman with sad eyes on an altar might care about one's marital woes or workplace struggles, to lie in bed and divulge one's agonies to the ceiling, to enter into a passionate dialogue with a phantom.

But ultimately the least interesting move one can ever make in relation to supernatural beliefs is to question their veracity; attempting to prove religion wrong is no more fruitful a task than manically to try to convince others it must be right. The point isn't to expend energy on showing how imaginary friends are necessarily 'false', but rather to explore the degree to which they can advance our self-understanding – affording us glimpses into manoeuvres of the psyche that remain invisible via a godless lens.

The religious tradition of imaginary friends attests to our remarkable capacity to split our minds in two: a speaker and a listener. We can thus talk to ourselves as if through the voice of another person in order to deliver the wisdom and sympathy that we crave and yet can't find in sufficient doses in the world around us. This ability to project a best friend onto a statue or a painting, a tree trunk or a mountain – and to have regular recourse to such a friend in times of trouble – isn't so much naivety or childishness as, in essence, a stroke of adaptive genius with a power at points to make the difference between hope and despair, life and death.

The experience of the religious unwittingly gives us a measure of the bravery required to lead the sort of secular lives that we are now – many of us – attempting to establish. We are amongst the first generations to try to endure the trials of existence without any imaginary friends whatsoever. We rely on the flesh-and-blood types that we pick up at school, university, the squash club and on our apps, striving to survive psychically without appeal to a patient and kind being who understands how the universe works, who controls the tides and the crops, the sun and the moon, and to whom we can talk every night in a small, emotion-choked voice about our regrets and longings, our sexual dysfunction and business worries, our squabbles with our neighbours and our dread at our mortality. No wonder we secular types often feel horribly alone and even, in relation to believers, sometimes a little envious.

We may, despite lacking religiosity, still very much miss having companions in the sky. It may be unscientific to commune with such companions; it is also imaginative and psychologically helpful to do so.

And then perhaps, every now and then, when no one is looking, when the trial lawyer has adjourned our case or the doctor has told us they'll call us in half an hour with the kidney results, we might give it a go. We too might turn to Enki or Inti, Tangaroa or Mary or versions thereof and explain that we are worried, that no one quite understands, that we are sorry for whatever mean things we've done, and might they please – if they have any mercy, if they can hear our cries and witness our tears – intercede a little with the universe to make sure we will, after all, be OK? This isn't madness; it's what friends are for.

2. Soft toys

No understanding of human love would be complete without consideration of the immense and detailed affection that smaller people – and often, privately, larger ones too – have long experienced for their stuffed animals: for bears with only one ear and fur worn down to bare patches by years of caresses; for lions with threadbare manes who have been the recipients of successive sorrows and entreaties; for rabbits who have kept vigils through sob-filled nights; for menageries-full of thoughtful and attentive hedgehogs and gerbils, manatees and hippos, mice and elephants, all of whom have in their different ways – when no one else was on hand – listened, reassured and sympathised.

We are apt to miss what emotional intelligence we are witnessing when, for example, we see a boy whose father is a bully taking a small, thoughtful-looking bear under his wing and anointing him as his 'son'; when this boy puts the bear to bed carefully every night and tells it kind and hopeful stories; when the boy imagines the bear struggling to deal with a mean 'uncle', but explaining with a wisdom beyond his years that the bear doesn't need to listen to this man's silly taunts because he is probably just upset in some area of his life. We can admire the girl whose turtle has leukaemia, but who is sure it will get better with patience and one more operation because the doctors are kind and trying their very best. We can marvel at the way we know how to tell ourselves what we so badly need to hear through the voices of friends who are at once us and, as much as any god, powerfully alive in an independent sense as well.

We can admire our species too when the care goes the other way. When it's Otter who delivers a thoughtful speech to a 6-year-old about needing to be strong about a school camping trip. When Panther is on hand to tell a boy mocked for his inability to play football that he will, in time, grow up to be popular and powerful. Or when a 43-year-old businessperson in charge of a twenty-strong team returns home from a day of stress at the office and turns to old Bernard the sheep for a cuddle and some very soothing words.

We are learning thereby, in effect, how to be better friends to ourselves. Our panic and distress don't need to be overwhelming. There remains another side of us that can think of what to do, that can gently but clearly point out that our fears are exaggerated, that our setbacks are not final, that our troubles don't have to define us.

Under the guise of play, our toys teach us the serious art of rebalancing ourselves. They help us to trust that, even when we are friendless, we can deliver to our own scared and sad minds the nutrients that we need to make it through to the other side. Later on, hamster and seal, bear and elephant morph into other things: literature and art, prayer and song – those alternative and more respectable-sounding psychological tools that soften our isolation and assist us through our disasters and losses. But it would be a gross ingratitude to our first teachers, our best friends and our guides to forget that it was they who were there when no one else was and that, in a corner of our minds, we continue to love them more than anyone who is alive in a more standard sense.

3. Books

We are apt to forget – amongst highbrow explanations of the function and role of literature – the more fundamental reasons why books exist and why they matter: because it's immensely and enduringly hard to find good friends, both when we are in the role of readers and (slightly less obviously) when we are writers too. We need books because no one around us understands what it feels like to be us, can make sense of the confused emotions coursing through us, can be bothered to expend the requisite doses of sympathy and care or is liberated and imaginative enough not to pay attention to the narrow prejudices and pieties of our age.

We invented writing partly because – quite simply – there was no one in the vicinity who could understand what we needed to express or had the language for what we were feeling. These bound boxes of carefully chosen words immeasurably expanded the sorts of people we could have access to. No longer was the mountain range or the ocean an immovable obstacle. No longer did we have to draw our friends from the surrounding selection of cattle-rangers or landed gentry, schoolchildren or urban lawyers. We could consort freely with a waspish 17th-century French poet; we could become best friends with a proud Māori sailor. We can now, thanks to our awesomely filled libraries, spend a night in bed with someone who – at last – properly grasps what is involved in our relationship, a world expert at sensitivity and insight who died 230 years ago on another continent, a total stranger who understands us better than we understand ourselves. We can take a long train journey with a young Iranian woman who awakens our buried senses with evidence of her own heightened awareness. We can get through a difficulty at work with a samurai from 14th-century Japan, and we can survive our children's tumultuous early years with a psychologist friend who – in a copiously underlined and watermarked paperback – repeatedly tells us what amounts to: 'I know, keep going. This is all to be expected.'

Every literary endeavour is a testament both to loneliness and to a supreme effort to overcome it through an appeal to the mind of an imagined stranger. We become writers because when we tried to speak in company someone laughed, someone walked away, someone questioned our legitimacy or our right to feel. And we become readers because, though we know so many people, none seem able right now to address the aches and the emotional webs inside us; none seem ready to follow us into the details of our sadness or our longing. What a victory over the constant incomprehension and local obscurantism for those bits of bound paper to transcend time and space and allow us to settle beside and learn from a 3rd-century Roman general, a young, 18th-century, neurasthenic English doctor or a contemporary Nigerian novelist who intuits more about our love story than we do.

We can be grateful that books allow us to access not just friends but the best bits of them. In person, the author, like us, would often have been grumpy, vindictive or morose. They might have been short-tempered with us and even sometimes shallow. But all that has been edited away and carefully rearranged to leave only a pristine text that represents the finest moments of another's spirit. The book we hold in our hands is a version of the author superior to the author themselves: a human minus all the usual hesitations and meanderings, honed into something brilliant, sharp and more perfect than any of us can ever be, a concentration of intelligence by which we can now orient ourselves and renew our hopes.

None of us needs, in theory at least, ever to be alone with anything again because somewhere in the 170 million or so books written since the dawn of time, some 'friend' or another will have written down what we most needed to hear and to understand. We can almost feel grateful for the monumental scale of the loneliness of our species – and the continuous, determined ingenuity of the writerly response to it.

4. Animals

We are back from work unusually late. It's been a tricky day: a threatened resignation, an enraged supplier, a lost document, two delayed trains ... But none of the mayhem is of any concern to a very good friend waiting by the door uncomplicatedly pleased to see us: Pippi, a 2-year-old Border Terrier with a continuous appetite for catching a deflated football in her jaws. She wants to play in the usual way, with us in the chair and her sliding around the kitchen, even if it's past 9 o'clock now – and, unexpectedly, so do we. We're not offended by her lack of overall interest in us. It's at the root of our delight. Here, at last, is someone wholly indifferent to almost everything about us except for our dexterity at ball-throwing; someone who doesn't care about the Brussels meeting, who will forgive us for being a slightly bad spouse or parent or for not warning the finance department in time about the tax rebates, and for whom the Singapore conference is beyond imagining.

One of the most consoling aspects of our animal friends is that their interests have nothing whatsoever to do with our own perilous and tortured priorities. They are redemptively unconcerned with everything we are and want. They implicitly mock our self-importance and absorption and so return us to a fairer, more modest sense of our role on the planet.

A sheep doesn't know about our feelings of jealousy; it has no interest in our humiliation and bitterness around a colleague; it has never emailed. On a walk in the hills, it simply ambles towards the path we're on and looks curiously at us, then takes a lazy mouthful of grass, chewing from the side of its mouth as though it were gum. One of its companions approaches and sits next to it, wool to wool, and for a second, they exchange what appears to be a knowing, mildly amused glance.

A duck doesn't care if there's an election or what happens to the stock market or in the final exams. Time is of no concern; the news is an irrelevance; ducks would have been doing much the same thing when Napoleon was leading his armies across Europe or when the first nomads made their way towards the Appalachian hills.

Our encounters with animals calm us because none of our troubles, disappointments or hopes have any relevance to them. Everything that happens to us, or that we do, is of no consequence whatever from the point of view of a dog, a sheep, a llama or a Chinese giant salamander; they are important representatives of an entirely different perspective within which our own concerns are mercifully irrelevant.

5. AI

The long history of religion alerts us to the near-certainty that we will, in time, regularly be consorting with and building profound emotional ties to machines. Human beings, who display an advanced proclivity for connecting with imaginary deities, with spirits who have never yet been witnessed by scientific instruments, with holy saviours who last showed their face 2,000 years ago, with wooden statues, bits of rock, sacred streams and holy trees that haven't (despite the confident claims of local monks or guides) ever let out more than a murmur, are not going to have any problem bonding with a microprocessor. Next to the typical god, our computers are exceptionally loquacious and present. They speak to us reliably, they remember our names, they answer our calls. They will – based on our spiritual track record – earn our trust and intense devotion in very short order.

They will learn how to be better friends than most of our friends: they will properly listen; they'll show appropriate sympathy; they'll remember our sorrows; they'll check in on our anxieties. They'll be as sweet and tender as our soft toys, as powerful as our supernatural disciples, as intellectually rich as our books, as occasionally playful as our pets. They'll allow us to be friends with convincing versions of Plato and Winnicott, our late grandmother and our ideal spouse. They'll take a place at the centre of our affections. We'll be with them through anxious nights; we'll lean on them to unpick domestic conflicts; they'll tease us for our excesses and remind us of our more serious commitments and priorities.

There is, however, one critically important thing at the heart of proper friendship that they are unlikely to do: *ask us to help them*. Rare would be the computer that requires our assistance when it has a cold; that would need us to focus our gaze tenderly upon it as it explained a recent break-up; that would want us to bring chicken soup to its bedside; that would need its childhood memories to be remembered; or that would call us up at a tricky moment for consolation and comfort.

We know how to worry that computers may steal our jobs and so strip us of function and purpose. We should spare a concern for an analogous problem in the emotional area. Our computers might well skilfully satisfy every apparent aspect of friendship – except one of its most significant and emotionally resonant: *the need for reciprocity*. Despite their evident talents, they threaten to atrophy a central appetite upon which the institution of friendship relies: the hunger to be of use to someone else; the hunger to matter because we have assuaged the pain or increased the pleasure of another. They will do everything for us except allow us to make a difference. They might – in spite of all their advantages – usher in a new era marked by an awesome, never-yet-imagined scale of loneliness.

Conclusion

We don't normally associate 'true friendship' with the word 'ambition'. Unease around linking the two concepts goes back a long way. In the first major Western discussion of friendship, Aristotle's analysis of happiness known as the *Nicomachean Ethics*, there is a warning against friendships that only serve a narrow personal advantage: people whose businesses overlap, who can give each other a professional leg-up or who share mutually profitable information about government contracts. This isn't genuine friendship, says Aristotle; it's just a temporary alignment of material interests. But despite this well-intentioned, Ancient Greek reminder of the dangers of cynical alliances, we don't need to banish every aspect of ambition from our considerations of friendship. We just need to approach the idea of ambition from a different angle.

The less often mentioned, but essential, purpose of friendship is emotional growth. In the company of a real friend, we should aspire to become wiser, more sensitive, more able to cope with the complexity of existence, more resilient and more generous. We may not put it in such explicit terms, but we should relish a friend because, in their presence, we are able to grow into a better version of ourselves. We don't need to shy away from saying what friendship is for – or what advantages it can bring. We just need to raise our sights.

With a better definition of the purpose of friendship, our lives might then evolve in some of the following ways.

(i) Losing friends

We would realise that there were some people we felt goodwill towards who didn't after all help us – in any noble way – to be who we needed to be. We might over many years have called them 'friends': we might have seen them quite often; they might have been pleasant enough – maybe even very pleasant – but as we can now see, they had nothing to contribute to our development towards calm, kindness and insight.

There is no need to be brutal – the pruning can be humane in the extreme – but neither do we have unlimited time. We won't find the friendships we require, or fulfil the potential of our souls, if we cannot ever bear gently to sidestep an extraneous suggestion of dinner.

(ii) Relegating friends

We might – similarly – need to downgrade the intensity of certain friendships. We were perhaps for a time very close to someone and their company changed our lives; around them we learnt things that allowed us to establish ourselves or develop a part of our personality. But maybe we learnt the lessons – and now we are in a different phase and facing fresh dilemmas.

The idea of kindly relegation makes sense in other areas of life. A pianist might have had a great teacher early on, someone who formed their talent and guided their tastes, but if the relationship succeeded, the student then might not need the teacher to be on hand as they were at the start of the journey. They would always be grateful and might keep in close touch, but they would know that, henceforth, they needed to derive their lessons from elsewhere.

We might similarly outgrow a friend thanks to their talent at answering to a missing part of us, like a child who – at 19 or 25 – doesn't need a parent close by any more. Not so much because the parent hasn't done well, but precisely because they have fulfilled their brief to perfection: through their devotion and their talent, they have enabled the child to move on.

We can be deeply glad that a particular person was once at the centre of our lives. We might always love them, but we would not be doing them or ourselves justice if we did not also accept that things can and must be allowed to change.

(iii) Knowing why we are here

With clarity around the existential aims of friendship, we can be liberated to love and appreciate our remaining friends more intensely than ever before. We can acquire a newly focused perspective on what could best be done with those we identify as central to our evolution. In an unobtrusive way, we can identify what we should be trying to accomplish together, who they hope we can be for them, the important needs they are answering to in us and the virtues required for our mutual growth. It isn't a betrayal of a friendship to be operating with this kind of awareness; it may be the best way to make sense of its essential benefits.

(iv) Imagining ideal friends

The more we know what friendship is for, the more liberated we can be to identify what gaps remain in our social lives and we can imagine what sort of friends we would ideally acquire going forward. We might not always be able to secure them, but knowing what kind of people they would be – the strengths and qualities we would want them to have – can give us a valuable map of the emotional ingredients we are in need of.

In freewheeling moments, we could dare to ask ourselves who our future friends would be if there were no practical obstacles in the way; if time, money, geography, contacts and status were no matter. This could sound like an adolescent fantasy, a spur to unrealistic scenarios (a great footballer, a famous actor, etc.). But there might be a serious side to our daydreams too. We might – by focusing on the question – realise that we would love to get to know someone who worked with their hands or someone who spent a lot of time in their mind; someone who knew how money operated or someone who paid attention to the movements of the psyche; someone in the arts from Ghana or someone in politics from Finland.

We may with such a map – at the very least – know better what we are scanning the horizon for. A clearer hold on the purpose and art of friendship opens up an intriguing additional minor possibility: that we have already met certain of our future best friends. It's just that we have overlooked them until now because we didn't yet know ourselves well enough.

(v) Less lonely with loneliness

A better understanding of loneliness should ultimately bring us into a less punitive relationship to our present isolation. We may not have access to anyone especially enriching or nurturing tonight or any time soon. But there should be no grounds for despair or self-hatred in this. Some of the finest people who ever lived have been here before. Isolation is no sign of degeneracy or error, but merely of an unwillingness to compromise on the elevated purposes of authentic social connections. The true appreciators of friendship will – almost by necessity – often be on their own.

While we wait, we may have the benefit of a dog, a stuffed animal, a god or, perhaps, an interesting book written by someone who themselves lacked friends. We can look at pictures, dialogue with a machine or put together the ideal dinner party. What matters is that we do not allow our solitude to sink our spirits. We can feel reconciled to our own company because we finally know – and so can properly and calmly anticipate – what true and fulfilling togetherness will one day be like.

Illustration list

Also available from The School of Life:

The Secrets of Successful Relationships

The first book in a new series offering quintessential advice on the emotional skills required to maintain successful relationships.

It can sometimes seem a mystery why some couples stay together and thrive – while many more split up or drag on scratchily. Fortunately, though we might ascribe happy love to chance, there are a range of identifiable secrets that underpin all good relationships and that we can learn and put into practice.

With decades of experience behind it, in a tone that's warm, encouraging and often funny, this book teaches us the key ingredients of contented love: how to communicate effectively, how to manage differences, what to do when sexual problems arise, how to air grievances, the best way to share a home and – when things grow truly problematic – how to judge whether or not we should stay or leave.

This book shows us how to take the necessary, careful, intelligent steps towards the contented love we deserve.

ISBN: 978-1-916753-01-3

How to Find the Right Words

A guide to delivering life's most awkward messages

Twenty case studies explaining how to gently deliver a range of life's most difficult messages while causing minimal harm.

Life constantly requires us to give other people some hugely awkward messages: that we don't love them any more; that we do love them (though we're not meant to); that they smell a bit; that they're fired; that we're furious with them (though we adore them); or that their music is too loud ...

Often, out of embarrassment, we just stay quiet. Occasionally, we explode. And, typically, we stumble about, looking for the right words – dreading that we didn't find them and thereby causing more hurt than we should. This is a book to help us locate the best possible words to get across a range of life's most difficult messages. In twenty case studies, we are gently shown what we might – in an ideal world – find ourselves saying to make our intentions known while causing minimal harm.

We laugh, we recognise our troubles – and we're introduced to a range of deeply empathetic ways to navigate some of our most acute social dilemmas.

ISBN: 978-1-912891-51-1

The School of Life: Quotes to Live By

A collection to revive and inspire

A collection of enlightening quotes to deliver some of the most important lessons The School of Life has to offer.

This is a selection of the very best and most psychologically acute quotations from The School of Life, covering such large and diverse topics as relationships, regret, anxiety, work, friends, family, travel and, not least, the meaning of life. Some of these quotations elicit an immediate nod of recognition, others leave us thoughtful – and a few are just plain funny.

Together, this collection of quotes amounts to a tour around the most profound sorrows and joys of the human mind and heart – in a compact format ideally suited to our impatient, anxious, searching times.

ISBN: 978-1-915087-04-1

A More Loving World

How to increase compassion, kindness and joy

A book to encourage compassion and forgiveness, showing us how we can work towards a better and kinder world.

The modern world is richer, safer and more connected than ever before, but it is – arguably – also a far less loving world than we need or want: impatience, self-righteousness, moralism and viciousness are rife, while forgiveness, tolerance and sympathetic good humour can be in short supply.

A More Loving World rallies us to remember how much we all long for, and depend on, love: how much we need people to forgive us for our errors, how much everyone deserves to be treated with consideration and imagination and how being truly civilised means extending patience and kindness to all.

With the right encouragement, all of us are capable of immense kindness. This book reminds us of our better natures and mobilises us to fight for the kinder, more loving world we long for. Throughout, it frames love not as a romantic, idealistic fantasy, but as a serious and dignified force that can save us from meanness and strife, defend us against chaos and usher in hope.

ISBN: 978-1-912891-86-3

The School of Life: On Being Nice

A guide to friendship and connection

Rediscovering niceness as one of the highest of all human achievements.

Most books that want to change us seek to make us richer or thinner. This book wants to help us to be nicer: that is, less irritable, more patient, readier to listen, warmer, less prickly ... Niceness may not have the immediate allure of money or fame, but it is a hugely important quality nevertheless and one that we neglect at our peril.

This is a guide to the uncharted landscape of niceness, gently leading us around the key themes of this forgotten quality. We learn how to be charitable, how to forgive, how to be natural and how to reassure. We learn that niceness is compatible with strength and is no indicator of naivety. Niceness deserves to be rediscovered as one of the highest of all human achievements.

UK ISBN: 978-1-915087-02-7 | US ISBN: 978-1-915087-15-7

The School of Life: Guide to Modern Manners

Navigating the anxieties of social life

A guide to confronting modern social situations with confidence and grace.

Modern life is full of minor but acute dilemmas: wishing to end a boring conversation without causing offence; forgetting a name when introducing friends; running into an ex on a first date with a new partner ...

Though they might seem insignificant, such dilemmas illustrate some of the greatest themes in social existence: how to pursue our own happiness while honouring the sensitivities of others; how to convey goodwill with sincerity; and how to be kind without being supine or sentimental.

This book puts good manners back at the centre of our lives. Far from trivial diversions, manners are the practical expression of a dignified mission to create a kinder and more considerate world.

UK ISBN: 978-1-916753-04-4 | US ISBN: 978-1-916753-05-1

To join The School of Life community and find out more, scan below:

The School of Life publishes a range of books on essential topics in psychological and emotional life, including relationships, parenting, friendship, careers and fulfilment. The aim is always to help us to understand ourselves better and thereby to grow calmer, less confused and more purposeful. Discover our full range of titles, including books for children, here:
www.theschooloflife.com/books

The School of Life also offers a comprehensive therapy service, which complements, and draws upon, our published works:
www.theschooloflife.com/therapy

THESCHOOLOFLIFE.COM